Soundings

CW01425719

Issue 36

Politics and markets

FOUNDING EDITORS
Stuart Hall
Doreen Massey
Michael Rustin

EDITOR
Jonathan Rutherford

MANAGING EDITOR
Sally Davison

ASSOCIATE EDITORS
Geoff Andrews
Sarah Benton

REVIEWS EDITOR
Jo Littler

ART EDITOR
Tim Davison

EDITORIAL OFFICE
Lawrence & Wishart
99a Wallis Road
London E9 5LN

ADVERTISEMENTS
Write for information to
Soundings,
c/o Lawrence & Wishart

SUBSCRIPTIONS
2007 subscription rates are (for three issues):
UK: Institutions £82, Individuals £35
Rest of the world: Institutions £92.50,
Individuals £45

Collection as a whole © Soundings 2007
Individual articles © the authors 2007
Cover photo © Martin Roemers, Panos Pictures

No article may be reproduced or transmitted by any
means, electronic or mechanical, including
photocopying, recording or any information storage
and retrieval system, without the permission in writing of
the publisher, editor or author

ISSN   1362 6620
ISBN   978 1905007 646
Printed in Great Britain by
Cambridge University Press, Cambridge

Soundings is published three times a year, in autumn, spring
and summer by:
Lawrence & Wishart,
99a Wallis Road, London E9 5LN.
Email: soundings@lwbks.co.uk

Website: www.lwbooks.co.uk/journals/soundings/contents.html

CONTENTS

Continued overleaf

Continued from previous page

SOUNDINGS SURVEY

Please note: there is still time to send in your completed surveys.
A copy is also available online at www.soundings.org.uk

Politics and markets

The market is constantly encroaching on our lives, and it increasingly pervades our politics too. The contributors to *Soundings 36* explore this issue in a number of different ways.

Ken Livingstone is one of the most interesting and creative politicians in Britain today. In his discussion with Doreen Massey he acknowledges the many ways in which business interests constrain his choices, but he argues that you can always find spaces within which you can make a difference. For example he has worked with business on a number of environmental initiatives. This kind of principled pragmatism raises the question of where you draw the line. Is promoting the flourishing of the City and its institutions an acceptable price to pay for keeping your place at the table of the powerful? Is the market so strong that we have to look to business for some of our partnerships for change?

While Ken Livingstone is guided by robust pragmatism, Erik Olin Wright puts forward an equally robust theoretical guide to transformative politics. His clarity about goals and practices is informed by a recognition of the conflict of interests that exists between any egalitarian project and commercial priorities. Thus, against the tendency within Labour circles to believe that there can be a politics without winners and losers, he clearly recognises that, for example, profit maximisation is incompatible with the kind of regulation that promotes the common good. This enables him to demarcate a politics that combines radical egalitarian democratic values with an institutional realism that avoids any blurring of the boundaries between markets and politics.

Jonathan Rutherford explores the many intellectual and institutional links between business and politics in his research on the web of connections between insurance companies, the academy and new government policies on welfare reform. He shows how US company UnumProvident's intellectual window-dressing for refusing sickness claims was welcomed into the government's own claims adjustment project. The psychology institute set up by the company employs former government personnel on its staff. The institute then produces monographs that - delivering a service for both the insurance business and the government - show that incapacity for work can be seen as a cultural phenomenon that can be addressed by a learning programme for the claimant. This is a classic neoliberal move - and Michael Rustin in his article shows how Richard Layard performs the same manoeuvre in suggesting cut-price individual therapy for depression, while simultaneously recognising that trends in society more widely are generators of mental illness. Sociological theories that are outdated and/or comply with the neo-liberal order are deployed to simplify the complex interrelationships between individual and society, allowing responsibility for social problems to be redefined as a problem for individuals.

Janet Newman and Nick Mahony, in their detailed response to the Compass publication *Democracy and the Public Realm*, look at a number of ways in which the language of democracy and participation is merging with the vocabulary of consumer choice. They also analyse the government's focus on civil society as an empty and apolitical space in which they can trawl for social entrepreneurs. They argue that civil society is becoming aligned with the market in new forms of hybrid organisations charged with service delivery and community renewal. In this way more public space is colonised.

Michael Rustin revisits the happiness debate, and argues that it is the prioritisation of economic growth over other values that is making people unhappy amidst their increasing affluence. Market values reduce people's happiness, as does the fear engendered by competition in our 'risk' society. New Labour's drive to remodel us all to fit the market and learn to compete increases our sense of insecurity. A reassertion of the social against the encroachment of the market is the best hope for greater well-being, and Mike is critical of the government's relentless requirement for individuals to take responsibility for increasing their performativity.

Richard Jones offers a user-friendly guide to nanotechnology in an article which explains its scientific underpinning but also explores its social context.

As he argues: 'If such a thing exists (or indeed ever existed) as an "independent republic of science", disinterestedly pursuing knowledge for its own sake, nanotechnology is not part of it.' Nanotechnology is fully integrated into the market for intellectual commodities, drawing universities into this market in their search for funds. It is at the heart of a shift towards goal-oriented science, where the focus is on products rather than exploration.

Valerie Bryson looks at the way time is colonised by neoliberalism. As she argues, as well as the long hours culture that afflicts many professional workers, and the many hours worked by the low-waged in order to earn enough to live on, the high levels of participation by women in the workforce are a main reason that people feel so short of time. There has been a shift of work from the household to the market economy, and this has meant non-market time has been taken away from us all. Increasingly, time means money and this is unhealthy for us all.

Faisal Devji discusses ways in which even the military in the USA, largely because of the contradictions involved in waging war on 'terror', are becoming culturally and institutionally fragmented. As he argues, this is signalled not only by infiltration into the military domain by private contractors and the CIA, but also by the spread of private or civilian practices among its own troops. Faisal quotes Donald Rumsfeld arguing for the US armed forces and Defence Department to promote 'a more entrepreneurial approach', to behave 'less like bureaucrats and more like venture capitalists'.

In the rest of the issue Nira Yuval-Davis argues that there is a need to be aware of different processes of racialisation in different historically specific situations. This applies particularly to Israel, which should be understood as a settler society, with all the implications that has for political resistance to Zionism. Iranian intellectual Ramin Jahanbegloo discusses the Iranian take on the liberal tradition with Danny Postel, in an interview which brings out some of the complexities of democratic universalism. And finally Cynthia Cockburn, in words and photographs, explores our discomfort and anxiety about death and the lifeless body.

SD

Soundings will develop the theme of politics and markets with a series of seminars on 'Cultures of Capitalism' that will begin in the autumn at Marx House in

Clerkenwell, London. The series is part of the left futures project. Readers can access the recent online debate at www.soundings.org.uk. The seminars will ask critical and strategic questions about contemporary changes in capitalism and modernity. What philosophical and theoretical resources do we need to create a counter-hegemonic politics to liberal market capitalism and its ideology of neo-liberalism? For further details see below and facing page.

Soundings

'CULTURES OF CAPITALISM'

SEMINARS

Marx House, 37a Clerkenwell Green, London EC1

The seminars will ask critical and strategic questions about contemporary changes in capitalism and modernity. The political defeat of the left has resulted in the dispersal of its language of social justice, freedom and equality. What philosophical, cultural and theoretical resources do we need to create new understandings of political and social transformation?

23 November 11am to 4.00pm
Cultures of capitalism

The new cultures of capitalism are colonising increasing areas of public life and the 'lifeworld'. In resisting this occupation, what is the role of symbolic meaning in making alternative cultures and politics?
■ *Stuart Hall, Jonathan Rutherford, Gilane Tawadros*

14 December 11am to 4.00pm
Re-imagining individual life

'Liquid modernity' and a consumer culture of distractions and the pursuit of wishes is reshaping individual life. How might the left respond with its own ethical values, forms of pleasure and ways of life?
- *Zygmunt Bauman (other speakers to be announced)*

18 January 2008 11am to 4.00pm
Understanding society and remaking politics

The new cultures of capitalism are transforming society and social relations. What sociological ideas do we need to understand the changes and develop a new politics of the left?
- *Beatrix Campbell, Michael Rustin, Richard Sennett*

22 February 2008 11am to 4.00pm
The financialisation of capitalism

Financialisation has become a dynamo of corporate profitability while being a source of grotesque inequalities and potential economic instability. What kind of political strategies might counter its impact on society and on local and global economies?
- *Doreen Massey (other speakers to be announced)*

Registration for each seminar costs £15, or £40 for a block booking of the whole series of four. It is advisable to book in advance as places are limited. Send cheque payable to Soundings, and details of the seminars you wish to attend, to FREEPOST, LON 176, London, E9 5BR (no stamp is needed).

Tickets available online from 10 September at www.soundings.org.uk.

Special offer: New standing order subscribers to
***Soundings* quoting code COC will receive free tickets to all the**
seminars on request (see page 10)

Further details from sally@lwbooks.co.uk or j.rutherford@mdx.ac.uk

RENEWAL compass
Soundings redpepper Middlesex University

Special offer to new *Soundings* subscribers

New subscribers filling in this standing order subscription form will receive free tickets to all four Cultures of Capitalism seminars.

To take advantage of this offer please complete the form below in BLOCK CAPITALS (photocopy is fine)

Please start my subscription to Soundings from issue 37. Please also send my 4 complimentary tickets for the Cultures of Capitalism Seminars.

To: _____ (your bank)

Bank's address: _____

Your account no: _____ Sort code: _____

Name of account holder: _____

Please pay by standing order to the account of Lawrence & Wishart at National Westminster Bank, Stockwell, London SW8, sort Code 60-20-31, account number 64716465, the sum of £35.00 immediately and £35.00 annually thereafter on September 1st each year.

Signed: _____ Date: _____

Your name: _____

Address: _____

Postcode: _____ Email: _____

Offer code: COC

Please return form to:
Soundings, FREEPOST, LON 176, London E9 5BR (no stamp needed)

The world we're in

An interview with Ken Livingstone

Ken Livingstone *talks to* Doreen Massey *about London as a global city, and how times - and politics - have changed since the GLC of the 1980s. On the one hand, London is now a place unrivalled in its particular form of multiculturalism. On the other, it is thoroughly entangled in the production of the contradictions of the current world order. How can a city respond to such a positioning?*

We meet in Ken's office, on the eighth floor of City Hall, and are still just chatting, before we get to the interview proper, when Ken rushes from the room and comes back waving a document. The old energy and enthusiasm have clearly not dimmed. 'Look', he says, 'look at this ...'

We are planning to launch this on 27 February.[1] It's a carbon reduction strategy for the city up to 2025/30. And it can all be done. You could actually get a 60 per cent reduction in emissions. And it's all based on behaviour changes and existing technologies. *All it requires is will.* [We pore over a succession of graphs and figures, his finger jabbing home with conviction the point that this can be done.] By 2030 we could get carbon emissions down to a level at which there isn't a problem at all. The only problem is political will.

---

1. *The Mayor's Climate Action Plan.*

So how do you generate political will?

Ah ... Well, it's plugging away endlessly on these things. Winning the argument, pushing it all forward. I meet at least a government minister a week, and I have done for the last six and half years. You make painfully slow progress - and then every now and then you get set back by them saying something like we need a new runway at Heathrow.

London is a fantastically important political voice in the country - I mean the GLC used itself like that. Do you see yourself in these big issues still as 'London', as a political voice in wider debates?

London has had this huge surge of growth and confidence, the whole world is fascinated by what London is doing, and has been for a long time. The Clinton Foundation is getting involved in all the climate change stuff with us, and helping to push that agenda forward. They have said there's only Chicago, Los Angeles and London close to doing anything like this, really, with New York coming up behind.

Is climate change the biggest priority now? There is a whole host of other stuff you've done.

Yeah ... but if you can't achieve the carbon emissions reduction I'm not certain human civilisation can be sustained. It's going to be catastrophic. I think the Stern report is the most optimistic he could have produced, because he is trying to lead business in that direction. The most sensible big capitalists recognise this issue. They have a long-term strategy for the firm, not just for the next five/ten years till the meltdown. At the time of the GLC, the international political divide mirrored the class divide in virtually every society, and business was totally signed up behind Thatcher - including her attacks on the GLC. But big business is now a strong ally on a whole range of fronts - climate change, improving skills in the workforce, investment in public transport and so on. Small business is still pretty poujadist, but a substantial percentage of the London workforce work for a relatively small number of large firms. This is not to say that the small/medium-sized enterprises are not important in their own way, but if you're doing deals with big business - in terms, say, of the affordable housing agenda, which we managed to get the developer community to sign up for, or the idea that every development must have 10 per cent renewable energy (now they're moving up to 20) - your problem is not big businesses. They're not the enemy anymore; it's all councils (and Labour ones are every bit as parochial as Tory and Liberal ones). And it's government, which is so terrified of what the *Daily Mail* will say.

Absolutely, whereas your forte has always been not being terrified.

Just ignore them.

Beyond climate change, have you got an overall view? ... You speak a lot about making London a sustainable world-class global city. When we were in the GLC we were definitely there to stop London turning Thatcherite and to be a voice against Thatcherism ... Is there an equivalent positioning now?

We were pushing the alternative economic strategy then. And we were still effectively presiding over the old Abercrombie plan for managing London down from 8.5 to 6 million. And that has all completely gone into reverse. Now it's about containing as much as possible of England's growth in London and on brown-field sites. The density of housing has increased by 300 per cent per hectare in four years. Basically we're driving Richard Rogers's urban taskforce approach - that what you need is real levels of density in order to make the city work. And given that the majority of the world's population now live in cities - it'll be three-quarters by mid century - you've got to find ways in which the cities can work sustainably. That means challenging a lot of those old perceptions we had on the left about the little home with a garden. Coming out of all the great slum clearance, that used to be the Labour councillor's goal.

Then there's the question of structure. In the GLC we did everything possible to prevent the decline of manufacturing, and nothing whatsoever to encourage finance and business services. Coming back to the job after a fourteen-year gap, that battle had been well and truly lost. Finance and business services had doubled in size and accounted for over a third of London jobs, and manufacturing was down to 300,000 and still declining - and most of that manufacturing was printing. And so you are now presented with a situation - certainly not one you would have chosen - in which finance and business services just drives the whole London economy, and now produces more wealth than the whole of British manufacturing. The clear thing that unleashed this was Thatcher's Big Bang. Before that London's financial centre was this small inward-looking club of old white men who'd all been to the same schools; she destroyed them, they were swept aside by international capital, which is much more dynamic, much more progressive, less racist and sexist (I mean, it's not wonderful in there, but compared with the old lot …); and the new people were quite prepared to engage with me, whereas that lot would refuse to meet. Now they recognise that mayors can deliver things, and they rely on me to try and get the flow of office development and new housing.

And there's also now this question of skills - all the old white and black working-class men who got left behind by the collapse of manufacturing at the docks and the arsenal have never really been fully re-engaged in employment. Particularly around the East End, where there's only about 55 per cent of the adult workforce in employment as opposed to 75 per cent nationally. As well as lifting London's skills base to keep in competition with New York, Shanghai, Tokyo and so on, you've also got to have a second-chance programme - it won't get all of them back, but it can give some of them the skills to get them back into employment. Some of these people haven't really had a secure job since the collapse in the 1970s. And 80 per cent of all the jobs coming to London in the next decade will be in finance and business services, and therefore if you aren't literate and numerate, and can't work in the office environment, you're in real trouble. There is also a creative layer of industry, which we are really looking to encourage … and which leavens the whole pattern. Then there are all the poorly paid jobs in the service sector and tourism and so on, where the London Living Wage is important, because you can lift them from being intolerable jobs and just not worth doing, to being just about worth doing. Telco led this demand and then we put one of the team on it.

In complete contrast to New Labour, who spin everything, distort everything, the core of people around me work on the assumption that we must tell the truth, because, given where our policies are coming from, if our facts don't stand up we have no impact at all. You've actually got to win the argument. The GLC became incredibly popular because we won the argument about abolition, that it wouldn't work. And so you never make a short cut. What is amazing is that when I was elected Mayor there was no London economic data.

So there had been nothing done since the LIS?[2]

No - people would take what the national figures were and try and abstract out what it might have been for London. We've now assembled a real body of knowledge about the London economy.

So far the two things you have really concentrated on are the City - and we'll come back to that - and climate change. When you talk about London being a world city or a global city what do you mean by that?

Well, it's quite clear that London has caught up as an equal with New York.

In terms of?

In terms of finance and business services, but also in terms of how it is perceived by the rest of the world - lots happening here, more young people choosing to come here than will go to New York and so on. And the other big dramatic change is that the black and Asian population has doubled since the GLC days. Thirty-five per cent of the workforce were born abroad, and 80 per cent of all the extra people coming into employment in the next ten years will be black or Asian or other ethnic minority, and so you have created a city which might very well still be the capital of Britain, but is actually genuinely a global city.

In the sense of being the whole world in one city ...

Yes. You've got 300 languages spoken in London and 200 in New York - which probably has the second highest total. The big advantage we have over the other cities that are quite mixed is that the races and places mix much better here. One person in twenty is mixed-race, and that really isn't the case in New York. And therefore those ideas about the clash of civilisations and global terrorism just don't make sense. And the attempt by America, following the collapse of

---

2. *The London Industrial Strategy*, published by the GLC in 1985.

communism, totally to reassert itself and dominate the whole world and get the world to accept its agenda, its culture - that is doomed too. Just look at the way China and India are emerging. There is never going to be that dominant super-power again - and it will be a very difficult transition as America comes to terms with that.

Can I pick you up on something before we talk about that? The way you do multiculturalism is that it isn't a happy-clappy kind of thing ...

Oh god no, you don't have to like everyone ...

You've taken stands that have offended particular groups, for instance. Could you reflect on that? I think it's a different form of multiculturalism from what is usually talked about in the States for instance ...

Yes. In the States it's about a shared set of American values, and therefore people are defined as Italian-American or Mexican-American or whatever. And that's not what we have in London. Here we say this is a city in which all these people preserve their identity whilst participating in the city. Most folk do. Some decide they don't want to. I think it prefigures in some ways what the world could be - think of the concept in the Cold War of co-existence.

We now have in the world several major cultures - Islam, China/Confucianism, America's version of capitalism and the slightly softer European version. None of these can ever be predominant in the long term. They've got to learn to co-exist. And if you look at the growth rates now for China (everyone keeps saying Chinese growth has got to slow down at some point but it clearly hasn't), at some time between ten and twenty years from now China will overtake America, which will be an absolutely seismic shock for the American psyche - and also for white people everywhere. For the last 500 years white folks have basically run the whole world to their own convenience, and that world will be passing within a decade. Think: in fifteen years time the Presidents of America and China and the Prime Minister of India will meet in a room to decide the course of the world - which is why I am in favour of a United States of Europe - it would be nice to be in there you know. And it's to prevent the formation of this kind of alternative power base that, over the last fifty years, around the oil companies and the White House, every move towards some sort of Arab Republic or any sort of unification in the Arab world has always been ruthlessly undermined. All sorts of little statelets have been propped up to prevent that. Moving into this sort of world is going to be difficult for the neo-cons - for example having to try and absorb China, which they are never going to be able to do because of its strong culture.

So you're really explicitly against US hegemony in that sense, the neo-con version, the Washington consensus version …

I'm probably anti *any* hegemony … what we have a chance for here is for the world to decide what it likes in cultures, for people to choose which bits of somebody else's culture they can ignore and which bits they want to adopt, and so on.

Nonetheless, in the middle of all this, and accepting that the financial City now supports a lot of your strategies, London is still the place of production of a neoliberalism which has supported the Washington consensus and has produced all kinds of disasters of various sorts, and inequalities around the world.[3] You are quite explicitly against neoliberalism I take it, and you have said things to that effect, and yet it's the centrepiece of the London Plan. I don't want you to reconcile those things; I just want you talk about how you play those things together …

Within that, within what you call neoliberalism (I wouldn't say neoliberalism, I think I'd say globalisation, i.e. the globalised economy), you have good and bad. I mean you have got Esso in there denying climate change, but you've got BP and now even Shell coming along saying something's got to be done. Shell came to see me saying they'd given up on the British government doing anything on hydrogen fuel cells, they'd like to do work with me in London. Then they told me they'd established a Muslim workers group. If only you could get that out of a borough council. So there's all sorts of contradictions. It is not a Bush, Cheney, Halliburton military-industrial-complex that dominates all of this. There

---

3. See Doreen Massey, 'London inside-out', *Soundings* 32. For a wider exploration of this issue see Doreen Massey, *World city*, to be published by Polity Press later this year.

are factions that push backwards and forwards within it, like there were in the American establishment in the run up to the Cold War - when there were those wanting to avoid isolating Russia (basically the Roosevelt position) and the hard-liners saying it must be isolated and defeated.

So there's contradictions, or there's kind of cracks in the system, that you can work with ...

Yes. You really need to talk to the people in big business to ask why they deal with me. Take *The Economist* article about me in January. They go through all the left-wing things - Chávez, Cuba - and of course they don't like any of this, but then they acknowledge that I got elected twice as Mayor because I actually do deliver all these other things. And their conclusion is I'm 'repulsive and brilliant in equal measure' [*Economist*, 11.1.07]. This is a real dilemma for them. I have the dilemma of having to deal with institutions such as the big banks, which are responsible for problems like the huge debt burden. But they also have to deal with me. I keep popping up with Cuba and Venezuela, and doing everything possible to promote China so that it emerges as rapidly as possible to challenge the hegemony of the USA.

And the Oyster card is a classic example of the small ways you can change things. The Oyster card contract was a PFI deal. We got elected and there was this Oyster card scheme, which on paper looked a good idea, but it was only aimed at people who had monthly and annual season tickets. Poor people weren't going to get them ... it wasn't going to be used on the buses for instance. And so we had a really brutal struggle with the PFI consortia. It ended up with us saying, look, either this is going to be a smart-card system for everybody or we're just going to cancel the PFI. What they wanted was a smart-card for people who had monthly and annual passes/season tickets, so guaranteeing that the card users would have a level of income that would allow them to be used as a target for sales and marketing of other things. It came down to a point where, to show we were serious, I sent off to Moscow to get an alternative quote, for what the Moscow underground system would charge in giving us their smart-card. Then we got negotiations, the scheme has changed, and now it's for everybody. That's the margin in which we operate - as somebody once said, 'we disagree with 95% of what this Labour government's doing but 5% is the margin in which we live'.

OK, but it is still the case that you are backing the City and its penumbra of all kinds of business-service industries - whether or not you call them neoliberal …

Well, I'm also arguing that you've got to have your Tobin tax, and that I should have the power to redistribute wealth from the super-rich in London.

That's what I want to know about. Because another problem with the finance-led strategy is that London becomes also the high capital of inequality, and that has huge effects in housing policies, in …

Yes. But that's not the fault of big business, that's the fault of the Labour government. Basically it's quite clear that in London the gross earnings of that small elite, the 1 per cent, is so out of line that you can actually take quite a big extra chunk of tax out of that…

So why don't you argue for that?

I can't see an alternative. There's no way this government, or Gordon Brown, is going to give me the power to redistribute wealth in London, from the super-rich or big business. So I'm tied to a much less progressive tax structure than I had at the GLC - which was wonderful.

But why aren't you using London's voice to say 'look, the vast inequality, your refusal to deal with the super-rich, is causing huge problems for the "growth engine" of this country'?

We *do* do that. But it just doesn't get reported. We know that the inequalities of wealth are going to produce huge problems. And if you look at the best period of growth the global economy has ever had, it isn't what we're going through now. It was probably when we went through the post-war consensus, when there was a much stronger emphasis on redistributive taxation - which started to break down in the 1970s.

So you do say to the Labour government that we should be taxing the super-rich?

Oh yeah. But I don't waste my breath trying to persuade Gordon Brown. In all our debates we so often are saying how much more money we need … and this is only a problem because he won't allow me to redistribute wealth within the city.

Mind you, if you had a strategy that wasn't so focused on finance wouldn't that in itself be somewhat redistributive?

What else would it be focused on? Am I going to rebuild manufacturing? This is not the world you create, it's the world you're in. What, effectively, has happened with the growth of financial services in London is that it's driven land costs and house prices and the cost-base up to a level where nothing else can get off the ground.

And it increases inequality.

Yes. But given that it is now the biggest and most important source of jobs in London - and not just the people it employs directly but also in all the services - then you can't say you are going to stop that, because it would lead to a pretty catastrophic recession in London for some period of time. So it's a real problem. You do everything possible to build the industries in the creative sector, and try also to sit down and look at issues such as the London Living Wage and so on. But ultimately we're locked into that set-up. So there's this real contradiction - at the heart of an administration that's making a real case for international redistribution of wealth and power, I'm reliant on one what is probably the world's biggest concentration of global corporate power outside New York.

That's the point, exactly, and it's such an irony …

I know, but New York is the same sort of city. What's been really interesting is that - and this is a big difference between the time of the GLC and now - New York and London have grown to be virtually mirror images of each other in terms of employment structure. Both are cities where the population is growing, both are very diverse cities, and both are cities that in cultural terms have almost nothing in common with the hinterland of their nations. And both of them are at the nexus of administration of the globalised economy …

Exactly - so it's just a deep irony from your point of view?

Well, give me dictatorial powers and we would be in a position to do something about it. But the other problem in all this is that even if you did something in London, finance would simply shift to Paris or Shanghai. You've got to build global structures of progressives and Labour and Greens to tackle it. If suddenly the Labour government gave me independence so I could manage the whole thing, and I whacked up taxes, finance would just up and go elsewhere. But, fortunately for us, there would be problems for them in moving to other locations in Europe. Paris won't allow the Hausmann grand design to be swept aside for big modern buildings, and finance people don't like being stuck far out from the centre. And Frankfurt just doesn't have enough else going on. The real threat to London as a financial centre would have been if Germany had moved the financial district from Frankfurt to Berlin as well as moving the capital - then Berlin would have been our big threat. So, broadly, nothing's going to rival New York in their hemisphere, and we'll most probably stay ahead in ours. But it's quite clear that if the Chinese government should wish it to happen at some point in the future, Shanghai could displace Tokyo as the financial centre in the East. The world will probably sustain three big financial centres, and there will also be a growth of smaller ones around the world.

The other thing is that it's not just a question of what the left does. You've now got Bill Gates, who says 'I've made 35 million pounds, I can't spend it, I shall have to do something progressive with it'. And Warren Buffet, who came along and did the same thing. And now you've got Clinton running round persuading firms to donate cheap medical supplies to the third world … So you're suddenly getting a layer of mega mega capital also recognising that the world can't go on like this - and god knows what will come out of all this.

They do something different from you though. They do things to stop the problems looking so bad, whereas what I understand you to be about is actually trying to change how things work; it's not just elastoplast.

Nor, actually, is what Gates and Buffet and Clinton are arguing about climate change. The Clinton Foundation is now really driving this agenda forward. Clinton is negotiating with major companies to switch over to manufacturing energy-efficient traffic lights. The idea is to guarantee that Chicago and New York and London and Los Angeles will buy them, and hopefully Paris and Berlin, and therefore the price will spiral down so that you get a long-term effect. That sort of stuff is quite interesting.

In the Cold War, broadly speaking, in every conflict you would either be on the Soviet Union's side or America's; and, broadly, almost every domestic political issue also reflected that same divide. There were all these absolute certainties. And even when you didn't like the Soviet Union, you still knew that in the war in Vietnam they were on the right side, or in Angola or Mozambique ... But now it's really not that simple. There *are* corporations out there that are led by people who are so short-sighted and blinkered that they endanger the future of the world. But there are others that recognise that there's a catastrophe coming. And equally the left was generally quite disparaging about restraining growth; the renewal of the left has to be very democratic, unlike its past, and it has to be very green. The picture is more complex than in the past. But in fact, because global warming is such a catastrophic threat, it can't be resolved by the simplistic agenda of the neo-cons; it's got to involve sharing, planning, restrictions ... and thus inevitably this agenda has to be addressed through what have traditionally been left approaches.

Yes, yes. We have been talking about global alliances - that one city can't do anything on its own, and that if you decided to go against finance it would just go somewhere else (even though in fact it's difficult to think where in Europe it might go). You have actually been doing quite a bit on global relationships - you've already mentioned you've got loads of stuff going on with Cuba, China, Russia, Venezuela. Can you tell us something about this?

Well, the core in all of this is the emergence of China. In the Cold War, the very fact that there were two sides meant there was an awful lot of space in between in which small nations and various struggles could manoeuvre. And once the Soviet Union collapsed there was this huge advance by one side, coinciding with globalisation, the rolling back of the welfare state, and devastating reductions in people's pay and conditions all over the bloody world. And it's not until a superpower emerges with a different agenda that you can really dramatically roll that back. And what's interesting about China is that, although they've adopted their own form of capitalism, it really isn't a *simple* capitalism. Our initial view was that we would have a city to city link with Shanghai, but we rapidly realised that all the major corporate decisions are still cleared by the Party machine in Beijing. You have to be in both cities. And in all our dealings with the Chinese Communist Party leadership we could see that they are genuinely proud that they have lifted 200 or 400 million people out of poverty. And they are much cleverer than the old Soviet Union was because, instead of putting half their GDP into matching America's military might, they just buy billions of dollars every year, and the moment they are threatened by America they stop buying dollars. Without the Chinese buying dollars, interest rates in America would have to soar and you'd have a great recession. They are quite brilliant about that strategy - they have bought all these bloody dollars and they have got the American economy by the short and curlies.

So, what's London's role in this then?

Well, London's role is to do everything possible to encourage links - between what's emerging in China and India, the progressive forces in the West, progressive forces in Latin America and so on. We just play a role in encouraging, helping develop all that.

Sounds a bit like multi-polarity …

Yes, in a world of uni-polarity, multi-polarity seems like very heaven. This is a half-a-loaf strategy, it's not the world you would have created.

OK tell me about Chávez or Cuba, what's going on? The Chávez deal is a very clear one.[4]

Chávez is aware that I can't redistribute wealth. So he's charging us £20 million a year less for our oil for running our buses, and we use the money saved to, say, have half fares on the buses for everybody on benefits.

---

4. The cities of London and Caracas have signed an equal-exchange deal.

And that's because he knows you can't redistribute within the city? That's quite explicit?

Well, I explained that to him. And what we would then do is share with them our historical experience of managing a huge city. Caracas is in some ways like London in 1830 - half the people live in shanty towns. Basically, London was the first of the great world cities to run into the kind of problems that are generated by poverty and growth, back in 1800, 1810, as everyone was driven off the land and came here. We've had two hundred years of experience of how to unlock these problems: sewage, water, housing, education and all that. For example, in Caracas, because petrol is a penny a litre there is just permanent gridlock. I mean the radio says if you're driving today take sandwiches, take a book, take an ipod, because you might be stuck for four or five hours in this jam. Increasingly, ministers do helicopters from one side of the city to the other. We can offer things like our traffic-light system which is managed by super-computers because no one can think fast enough to do it any more ... And so we will open an office there and staff will be seconded there to work with Chávez's ministries.

So on the one hand you're teaming up with Chávez, and on the other hand you're going to Davos.

I'm going there to talk about what we're doing on climate change.

It's not an incompatibility or inconsistency.

No, though it might very well be that I'll catch a whiff of the tear gas and then ... but don't forget that one of the first things we did here was to crush the mad anti-globalisation protesters. We told people not to go on the demo, we penned them in.

Why did you do that?

Because these people are mad, they will destroy you - in exactly the same way as the ultra-lefts around in the shadows present you with nothing but risk, because they open you to attack from your opponents. I mean you can't have, in a city like London, two hundred people running up and down Oxford Street smashing windows, because it just creates the ground on which the right advance. Don't forget all those decades in which the Communist Party taught its cadres self-discipline. You don't go off and do mad gestures because you open the way for reaction. You move when you can advance.

But what about the wider counter-globalisation movement? You supported the World Social Forum.

Yes, all of that, but you've *got* to isolate and marginalise the violent fringe because they are most probably being funded by neo-cons anyhow. I mean, how many of the demos that went violent in the past in Britain had been infiltrated by agent-provocateurs, sent in there to make sure there wasn't a disciplined, organised march? I don't think it's *all* agent-provocateurs, but I think, since the collapse of Communism, there has been a whole generation of young people who are angry, but have grown up without the experience of going into Communist or Trotskyist organisations or trade-union movements. And because they haven't been trained and disciplined in Marxism and haven't learned from people who have told them that it is a lifelong struggle, they get really angry and go out and smash in a shop window. I'm sorry, but these people are a luxury we can't afford. I'm not going to be guilt-tripped by some angry 25 year old who in twenty years time will be a merchant banker and have forgotten it all. I've invested my entire adult life in trying to advance a socialist cause and I have stopped worrying about being guilt-tripped by people half my age who are just having a spasm.

Is there anything else you'd like to put into this interview?

No, no, no I never volunteer anything. It gets me into trouble!!

But you love getting into trouble! Anyway, thanks very much.

Guidelines for envisioning real utopias

Erik Olin Wright

Erik Olin Wright *offers insights into ways of thinking about alternative futures.*

To be a radical critic of existing institutions and social structures is to identify *harms* that are generated by existing arrangements, to formulate *alternatives* which mitigate those harms, and to propose *transformative strategies* for realising those alternatives. There was a time when many intellectuals on the left were quite confident in their understanding of each of these: theories of class and political economy provided a framework for identifying what was wrong with capitalism; various contending conceptions of socialism provided models for alternatives; and theories of class struggle and socialist politics (whether reformist or revolutionary) provided the basis for a transformative strategy. Today there is much less certainty among people who still identify strongly with left values of radical egalitarianism and deep democracy. While left intellectuals remain critical of capitalism, many acknowledge - if reluctantly - the necessity of markets and the continuing technological dynamism of capitalism. Socialism remains a marker for an alternative to capitalism, but its close association with statist projects of economic planning no longer has much credibility, and no fully convincing alternative comprehensive model has become broadly accepted. And while class struggles certainly remain a central source of conflict in the world today, there is no longer confidence in their potential to provide the anchoring agency for transforming and transcending capitalism.

This is the context in which there has emerged on the left a renewed interest in thinking about broad visions and imagining new ways of approaching the problem of alternatives to the existing social world. The recent publications of Compass are good examples of this kind of work.[1] Other examples include Michael Albert's effort at elaborating a comprehensive model for a participatory economy, christened Parecon; Gar Alperowitz's work, *America Beyond Capitalism: Reclaiming our Wealth, our Liberty and Our Democracy*; Roberto Unger's book, *What Should the Left Propose*; and the volumes published out of my project, *Envisioning Real Utopias*.[2] I call the problem of exploring alternatives 'envisioning real utopias' to highlight the inherent tension between taking seriously emancipatory aspirations for a radically more humane and just world, and confronting the hard constraints of realism. This is a difficult endeavour. It is much easier to be a realist about what exists than about what could exist, and much easier to dream of a better world without worrying about the practical problems of unintended consequences and perverse dynamics. But if we want to realise the values of egalitarian democracy in a sustainable way that creates the widespread conditions for human flourishing, then we must grapple with this tension.

In this essay I will elaborate five guidelines for these kinds of discussions of emancipatory alternatives to the existing social order:

◆ Evaluate alternatives in terms of three criteria: desirability, viability, achievability

---

1. *The Good Society*, Jonathan Rutherford and Hetan Shah (eds); *A New Political Economy*, Hetan Shah and Martin McIvor (eds), both Compass 2006.
2. Michael Albert, *Parecon: Life After Capitalism*, Verso, 2003; Gar Alperowitz, *America Beyond Capitalism: Reclaiming our Wealth, our Liberty and Our Democracy*, John Wiley, 2004; Roberto Unger, *What Should the Left Propose*, Verso 2005. Volumes in the Real Utopias Project: Joshua Cohen and Joel Rogers (edited and introduced by Erik Olin Wright), *Associations and Democracy*, Verso 1995; John Roemer (edited and introduced by Erik Olin Wright), *Equal Shares: making market socialism work*, Verso 1996; Samuel Bowles and Herbt Gintis (edited and introduced by Erik Olin Wright), *Recasting Egalitarianism: new rules for equity and accountability in markets, communities and states*, Verso 1999; Archon Fung and Erik Olin Wright, *Deepening Democracy: Innovations in empowered participatory governance*, Verso 2003; Bruce Ackerman, Ann Alstott and Philippe van Parijs (edited and introduced by Erik Olin Wright) *Redesigning Distribution: basic income and stakeholder grants as cornerstones of a more egalitarian capitalism*, Verso 2005; Janet Gornick and Marcia Meyers (edited and introduced by Erik Olin Wright), *Institutions for Gender Egalitarianism* (forthcoming).

♦ Do not let the problem of achievability dictate the discussion of viability
♦ Clarify the problem of winners and losers in structural transformation
♦ Identify normative trade-offs in institutional designs and the transition costs in their creation
♦ Analyse alternatives in terms of waystations and intermediary forms as well as destinations. Pay particular attention to the potential of waystations to open up virtuous cycles of transformation.

Desirability, viability, achievability

Social alternatives can be elaborated and evaluated by three different criteria: *desirability, viability,* and *achievability.* These are nested in a kind of hierarchy: Not all desirable alternatives are viable, and not all viable alternatives are achievable.

In the exploration of *desirability*, one asks the question: what are the moral principles that a given alternative is supposed to serve? This is the domain of pure utopian social theory and much normative political philosophy. Typically such discussions are institutionally very thin, the emphasis being on the enunciation of abstract principles rather than actual institutional designs. Thus, for example, the classical Marxist aphorism to describe communism as a classless society governed by the principle 'to each according to need, from each according to ability', is almost silent on the actual institutional arrangements which would make this principle operative. These kinds of discussions can be quite valuable, for they help to clarify the normative goals of projects of social change and help us evaluate whether or not we are moving in the right direction, but by themselves they tell us little about how to actually design institutions.

The study of *viability* is a response to the perpetual objection to radical egalitarian proposals 'it sounds good on paper, but it will never work'. The exploration of viability brackets the question of the political achievability of the proposed alternative under existing historical conditions, focusing instead on the likely dynamics and unintended consequences of the proposal if it were to be implemented. Two kinds of analyses are especially pertinent here: systematic theoretical models of how particular social structures and institutions would work, and empirical studies of cases, both historical and contemporary, where at least some aspects of the proposal have been tried.

The problem of *achievability* of alternatives is the central task for the practical political work of strategies for social change. It asks of proposals for social change that have passed the test of desirability and viability what it would take to actually implement them. This turns out to be a very difficult undertaking, especially because of the high levels of contingency of conditions in the future that will affect the prospects of success of any long-term strategy. Generally, as a result of this uncertainty, discussions of achievability tend to become quite short-term, focusing on existing configurations of social forces and potential political coalitions that can plausibly be persuaded to adopt specific projects of change.

Consider the example of unconditional basic income (UBI), a proposal that has gotten considerable discussion in recent years (for more discussion on this see the *Redesigning Distribution* book in the Real Utopias series). UBI is a proposal for a fundamental redesign of institutions of income distribution.[3] At its core UBI is a very simple idea: every citizen should receive a monthly stipend sufficient to live at a decent no-frills standard of living above the 'poverty line' without any conditions. The stipend goes to the rich and the poor, the advantaged and the disadvantaged, the industrious and the lazy. It is given unconditionally, without work or other requirements. Of course, to pay for a UBI taxes would have to be significantly raised on the rich and thus they would not be net beneficiaries - i.e. their additional taxes in a UBI regime would be higher than the UBI itself - but everyone gets the grant. The questions then are: would this be desirable, viable, and achievable?

There is a lively debate among philosophers and others about whether UBI would be desirable. Philippe van Parijs, one of the pre-eminent theorists of UBI, argues that it is justified on the grounds that it guarantees 'real freedom for all' by insuring that everyone has the capacity to make certain autonomous choices around their life plans. David Purdy argues that UBI is a crucial component of a transition to a sustainable, steady-state economy in which social development rather than economic growth is the central axis of economic activity and public

---

3. It is better to refer to UBI as a redesign of the institutions of distribution than to describe it as a mechanism of income redistribution. The expression 'redistribution' implies that there is something that can be called an income distribution which is generated by market mechanisms which is then redistributed through state mechanisms (taxes and transfers). This suggests that market-generated distributions are somehow pre-political, natural, spontaneous. In fact, the politically established rules of the game deeply shape the way markets themselves generate income and distribution. The market does not first produce an income which is then redistributed; the income generated by actors in an economy is from the start jointly shaped by market relations and political institutions and conditions. UBI is simply an alternative structure of distributive rules.

policy. Others have argued that it is desirable because it eliminates absolute poverty without creating poverty traps associated with means-tested programmes.[4] I have defended UBI on two grounds: first, it facilitates the expansion of non-commodified productive activity in a wide range of domains - care-giving, artistic production and performance, community building - by guaranteeing the participants in such activities a basic standard of living unconnected to market earnings, and second, it shifts the balance of power from capital to labour by giving workers greater bargaining power both individually (because of the option of quitting given jobs or exiting the labour market altogether) and collectively (because UBI functions as a permanent unconditional strike fund).[5]

The problem of viability of the proposal revolves around its impact on taxation and work incentives (for more on this see David Purdy's *Soundings* article). Sceptics argue, first, that tax rates would have to be so high that this would create large disincentives for investment; and second, too many people would opt to live on the basic income rather than seek income in labour markets. For both of these reasons the economy would not produce sufficient income to generate the taxes needed to sustain the basic income. Basic income would self-destruct. Defenders of basic income reply that both of these problems are greatly overstated. Since UBI would replace a vast array of targeted and means-tested income support programmes, and since it is administratively much simpler than the programmes it replaces and thus saves on administrative costs, the total cost of a reasonable basic income would only be moderately more than currently existing generous welfare state redistributive programmes. The labour supply objection is more difficult to assess for this depends very much on the specific preferences for material consumption and non-market activities (both leisure and productive non-market activities) in a population, but it is important to note that some of the non-market activities which would be facilitated by UBI would increase aggregate productivity by solving certain kinds of social problems, and thus even if they do not directly generate taxable income, they contribute

---

4. Philippe van Parijs, *Real Freedom for All*, Oxford University Press 1995; David Purdy, 'Citizen's Income: sowing the seeds of change', *Soundings* 35; Irv Garfinkle, Chien-Chung Huang, Wendy Naidich, 'The Effects of a Basic Income Guarantee on Poverty and Income Distribution', in *Redesigning Distribution* (op cit).
5. See 'Basic Income, Stakeholder Grants, and Class Analysis', in *Redesigning Distribution*; and 'Basic Income as a Socialist Project', *Basic Income Studies*, Vol. 1 No. 1, Article 12. Available at http://www.bepress.com/bis/vol1/iss1/art12.

to the income-generating capacity of the system.

In most developed capitalist economies, a generous UBI is not currently achievable: the dominant political forces in these countries do not back basic income as a general proposal, and public opinion is certainly not behind it. Nevertheless, there are grounds to believe that a coalition could potentially be constructed for such a proposal in the future. The key here is to recognise the ways in which UBI could significantly contribute to the solution of a heterogeneous array of practical political, economic, and social problems and satisfy a variety of different kinds of interests, and thus become a policy supported by a coalition of those who support it for moral reasons and those who support it for pragmatic reasons. For example, UBI could be a solution to the knotty problem of agricultural subsidies in developed capitalist countries. Agricultural subsidies are ideologically defended on the grounds that they are needed in order for small farmers to survive, but the form of these subsidies - directed at prices of crops and similar mechanisms - typically end up benefiting large farmers and corporate agriculture more than small farmers. Suppose that all of these direct farm subsidies were eliminated and a generous UBI introduced. This would enable small farmers to farm, since with a UBI they would not need to produce their basic income through farming labour; farming would serve only to generate discretionary income. Agribusiness, on the other hand, would receive no subsidy - and indeed, since agricultural labour is likely to become more expensive because of the improved bargaining position of farm workers, corporate agriculture might be hurt by the reform. UBI could thus be the basis for a coalition of interests between small farmers and artists, since for both of these social categories UBI makes it easier for people to carry out their preferred social activities by partially disengaging the problem of meeting their basic economic needs from earning income from their productive activity.

All three issues - desirability, viability and achievability - are thus relevant to the understanding of alternatives to existing social structures and institutions. At this point in history I believe that the most pressing intellectual task of these three is the problem of viability. In a sense, the problem of desirability unconstrained by viability and achievability is *too easy*: it is too easy to elaborate the moral principles and values we want to see embodied in alternatives and to show how these values are represented by various schemes. And the problem of achievability is *too hard*: there are simply too many contingencies and uncertainties for us to assign meaningful probabilities to the achievability of a given viable alternative very far into the future. The problem of viability is particularly important because there is so much scepticism among people who are convinced of desirability and willing to participate in the political work to make alternatives achievable, but have lost confidence in the workability of visions beyond the existing social order.

Achievability should not constrain discussions of viability

Discussions of the viability of new institutional designs that bracket the problem of the actual political achievability often encounter strong objections. What is the point, it is sometimes argued, of talking about some theoretically viable alternative to the world in which we live if it is not strategically achievable? There are two responses to the sceptic.

First, there are so many uncertainties and contingencies about the future that we cannot possibly know *now* what really are the limits of achievable alternatives in the future. The further we look into the future, the less certain we can be about the limits on what is achievable. Achievability is often determined by historically contingent windows of opportunity that open up unexpectedly rather than anticipated strategies understood well in advance. No one, for example, would have thought in 1985 that a destruction of the Soviet Union and the shock therapy transition to some form of capitalism was achievable within a decade. So, to let our firm knowledge of achievability constrain our analysis of viability would necessarily exclude discussions of some alternatives that eventually do become achievable.

Second, the actual limits of what is achievable depend in part on the beliefs people hold about what sorts of alternatives are viable. This is a fundamental if sometimes elusive point about the very idea of there being 'limits of possibility' for social change: social limits of possibility are not independent of beliefs about limits. When a biologist argues that in the absence of certain conditions, life is impossible, this is a claim about objective constraints. Of course the biologist could be wrong, but the claims themselves are about real, untransgressable limits of possibility that exist independently of our theories about those limits. Claims about social limits of possibility are different from these claims about biological limits, for in the social case the beliefs people hold about limits systematically affect what is possible. Developing systematic, compelling accounts of viable alternatives to existing social structures and institutions of power and privilege, therefore, is one component of the social process through which the social limits on achievable alternatives can themselves be changed.

For these reasons, the analysis of the viability of alternatives to existing institutions should not be short-circuited by the problem of political achievability. Of course, if it could be shown that in principle a given proposal could never be achieved under any conceivable conditions, this would reduce the interest in understanding its potential viability. Nevertheless, even in this extreme case, the discussion of viability could be productive insofar as it clarifies issues of the workability of institutional design, which might have implications for modified versions that could be implemented.

Winners and losers

In recent years, discussions of democratic egalitarian alternatives to existing institutions frequently argue that these alternatives are good for everyone, that they constitute 'win-win' solutions to existing problems. The appeal of a given proposal will obviously be greater if no one is really hurt by it. There are some passages in the Compass *Programme for Renewal* books that have this character. For example, in *A New Political Economy*, the authors argue that a democratically revitalised state 'can enter into continual negotiation with the market, to hold it in check, boost its performance and *save it from itself*' (p15, italics added); and that 'the good economy outperforms the deregulated "feral" economy in traditional economic terms' (p21). If it were the case that in order to save the market from self-destruction we would need the full package of democratic egalitarian transformations outlined in the *Programme for Renewal*, then this would mean that capitalists should support these transformations, for their survival as well depends on them. Similarly if it were indeed the case that the good economy actually outperformed the neoliberal economy in *traditional* economic terms - i.e. the good economy generated a higher rate of profit, greater competitiveness globally, more rapid accumulation of capital, etc - then, again, capitalists would do better under the alternative. Under these conditions their opposition, therefore, would not reflect their class interests but their stupidity and 'false consciousness'.

Now, there may be special circumstances in which policies which are best for society are also best for corporations, but in general serious democratic egalitarian institutional transformations are not optimal for capitalists and large corporations. While it is true that capitalism does best under *some degree* of regulation, it is generally not the case that the *optimal* level of regulation for the interests of corporate capitalism is the same as the optimal level for workers and ordinary citizens. One way of visualising this is illustrated in Figure 1. This figure shows the relationship between the degree of economic regulation of markets and firms and 'economic performance' as defined by the interests of capitalists and corporations, and as defined by the interests of ordinary people in the broader society. For capitalists, good economic performance serves their interests when it contributes to high and stable profits; for society as a whole, good economic performance serves interests of most people when it generates a high and sustainable quality of life. Since profit maximisation is generally facilitated by a certain amount of unemployment and insecurity among workers (since this reduces the bargaining power of employees) and significant negative externalities (since this reduces costs), it is generally the case that the optimal level of regulation for profit maximisation is lower than for the common good. Thus while it may be true that the radical deregulation proposed by neoliberals might be ultimately harmful for capitalists - it is below the optimal level of regulation for capitalism - it does not follow that the wide-ranging regulations of a democratic egalitarian project for the reassertion of societal control over the market would be good for capitalists.[6] By and large, powerful and wealthy individuals and corporations will be 'losers' in a meaningful movement towards democratic egalitarianism.

It is understandable that the idea of win-win is politically appealing, but it creates the illusion that the main problem egalitarian democrats face

---

6. It may also be the case, as I have argued elsewhere, that capitalists might even have good reason to prefer the sub-optimal levels of regulation of neoliberalism (in spite of its harmful effects) if they fear that, for political reasons, moving towards their 'optimal level' may open the door for more extensive regulation. (In Figure 1 the interests of capitalists are better served at the neoliberal level of regulation than at the socially optimal level of regulation.) This could be called the 'Frankenstein problem' for regulation of capitalism: building the levels of state competence and capacity to regulate capitalism optimally for the interests of capitalist corporations creates a state that is also capable of regulating it optimally for the society. Capitalists may fear creating a 'monster' they cannot control, and thus prefer the neoliberal solution even though it creates less than optimal constraints on the market for their economic interests. The capitalist optimum may not be a stable equilibrium.

Economic Performance

| Economic performance as defined by capitalist interests: profits, competitive advantage, etc. | Economic performance as defined by 'society': quality of life, environmental sustainability, high positive externalities and low negative externalities, etc. |

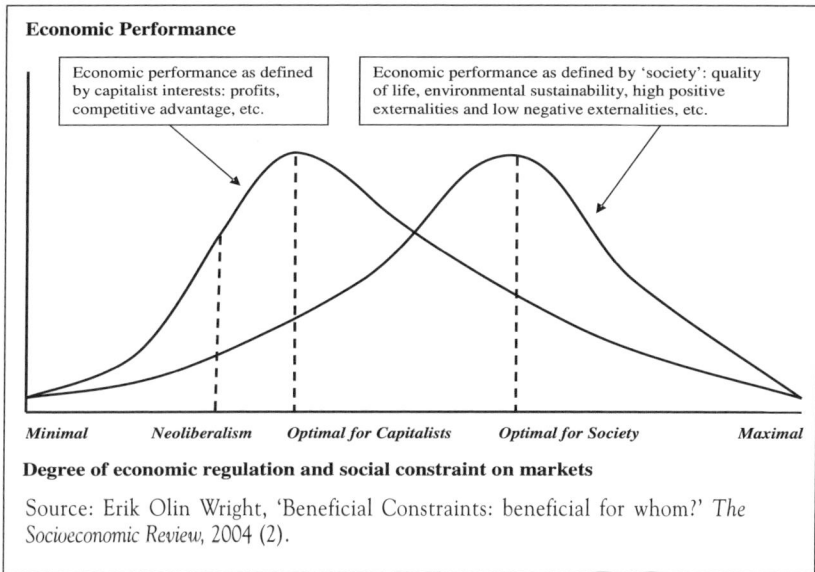

| *Minimal* | *Neoliberalism* | *Optimal for Capitalists* | *Optimal for Society* | *Maximal* |

Degree of economic regulation and social constraint on markets

Source: Erik Olin Wright, 'Beneficial Constraints: beneficial for whom?' *The Socioeconomic Review*, 2004 (2).

Figure 1 - The Relationship between the Degree of Regulation of Markets and Economic Performance

in confronting the power and privileges of elites and dominant classes is enlightenment, whereas typically the problem is defeating them politically. This does not mean - as revolutionary socialists assumed in the past - that serious advances in democratic egalitarianism necessarily require *destroying* capitalists' power altogether, but it does mean blocking off their preferred solutions, and this is a question of power, not just enlightenment. As Joel Rogers has put it in discussing the problem of creating the conditions for 'high road capitalism', the task is to 'close off the low road and pave the high road'. And closing off the low road requires political victories over opposition.

Normative trade-offs and transition costs

It is a commonplace in all political debates to claim that a preferred institutional transformation is better in all respects than the institution it replaces; that the transition from one to the other assures instant improvements; and that there are no important normative trade-offs and no transition costs to transformation. As in the claims for win-win solutions in which everyone is better off, such arguments may help to solidify support for the proposal. But this also opens to the door to disappointment and feelings of having been mislead when transition costs are real and trade-offs are encountered.

Consider, for example, the problem of the relationship between the degree of equality in an economy and economic growth. A standard argument by conservatives is that there is a sharp trade-off here: if income is redistributed from the successful to the unsuccessful (i.e. from the rich to the poor), then incentives will be reduced for investors, entrepreneurs, innovators and risk-takers, and as a result economic growth will be slowed. Egalitarians have correctly criticised this generic prediction by showing, for example, that it is not the case that economic growth is slower in those developed capitalist countries with less inegalitarian distributions of income, and that a high level of economic inequality brings its wake a host of social problems that are themselves efficiency-reducing (crime, social disorganisation, low morale, etc). Nevertheless, the data also do not support the strong claim that there would be no incentive problems for innovation, entrepreneurship and risk-taking if the full gambit of democratic egalitarian proposals were instituted. We just don't know, and the arguments that there might be such problems are plausible; there may indeed be a trade-off. This does not imply, however, that the trade-off isn't worth making. One might well decide, all things considered, that giving up a little incentive for certain kinds of entrepreneurial innovation is worth the improvement in the quality of life for the economically less advantaged. This is particularly the case if much entrepreneurial innovation driven by market competition and the prospects of large personal rewards is devoted to refined forms of consumerism - large home theatre video systems - rather than innovations that benefit the vast majority of people.

This particular trade-off problem is illustrated in Figure 2. In this figure, the rate of economic growth (the left hand vertical scale) increases as you move from extremely high levels of inequality to moderately high levels and then slowly declines, due to the reduced incentives for entrepreneurial risk-taking and the like. The long-term quality of life for the economically disadvantaged (the right hand vertical scale), however, continues to rise as inequality is reduced until you approach extremely low levels of inequality, where the slower rate of economic growth eventually undermines the long-term prospects for the disadvantaged. If this figure accurately portrays the trade-offs, then a good case can still be made for the relatively low inequality equilibrium on social justice grounds; but this is a trade-off, and it should be defended not denied.

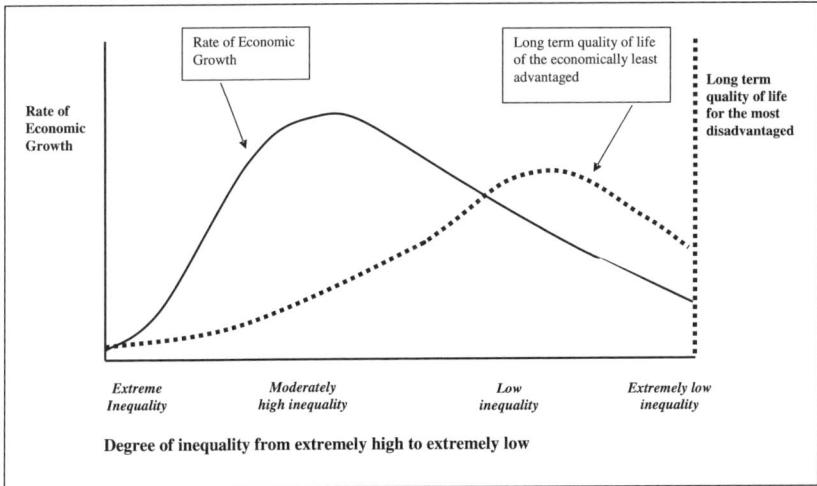

Figure 2 - Degree of Inequality, Economic Growth, and the quality of life of the disadvantaged.

The picture in Figure 2 is purely hypothetical. We don't actually know very much about what the long-term trade-offs might be in the economic and political environment of a well institutionalised democratic egalitarian society. The trade-offs might well be less than pictured here, or perhaps more. One important reason for explicitly acknowledging the potential for such trade-offs is to enhance the learning capacity in the process of building the new institutions. Simply because such trade-offs exist does not imply that additional institutional innovations might not help reduce them. If the political project of moving in the direction of radical democratic egalitarianism recognises the real possibility of these kinds of trade-offs, then the people involved in the trial-and-error process of democratic experimentalism are more likely to recognise the problems and work on ways of dealing with them. This is, perhaps, the most important role for social science in the long-term process of 'envisioning real utopias': enhancing the learning capacity of the participants in real world endeavours and making another world possible. And this requires as clear-headed an acknowledgement of dilemmas and trade-offs as possible.

Waystations

The final guideline for discussions of envisioning real utopias concerns the importance of waystations. The central problem of envisioning real utopias concerns the viability of institutional alternatives that embody emancipatory values, but the practical achievability of such institutional designs often depends upon the existence of smaller steps, intermediate institutional innovations that move us in the right direction but only partially embody these values. Institutional proposals which have an all-or-nothing quality to them are less likely to be adopted in the first place, and may pose more difficult transition-cost problems if implemented. The catastrophic experience of Russia in the 'shock therapy' approach to market reform is historical testimony to this problem.

Waystations are a difficult theoretical and practical problem because there are many instances in which partial reforms may have very different consequences than full-bodied changes. Consider the example of unconditional basic income. Suppose that a very limited, below-subsistence basic income was instituted: not enough to survive on, but a grant of income unconditionally given to everyone. One possibility is that this kind of basic income would act mainly as a subsidy to employers who pay very low wages, since now they could attract more workers even if they offered below poverty level earnings. There may be good reasons to institute such wage subsidies, but they would not generate the positive effects of a UBI, and therefore might not function as a stepping stone.

What we ideally want, therefore, are intermediate reforms that have two main properties: first, they concretely demonstrate the virtues of the fuller programme of transformation, so they contribute to the ideological battle of convincing people that the alternative is credible and desirable; and second, they enhance the capacity for action of people, increasing their ability to push further in the future. Waystations that increase popular participation and bring people together in problem-solving deliberations for collective purposes are particularly salient in this regard. This is what in the 1970s was called 'nonreformist reforms': reforms that are possible within existing institutions and that pragmatically solve real problems while at the same time empowering people in ways which enlarge their scope of action in the future.

***

The Compass *Programme for Renewal* is an important contribution to revitalising a sense of alternatives to the market-centred hypercapitalism of neoliberalism.

Its value is not so much in the specification of a concrete set of specific policy proposals for Britain in the present - although it does contain a range of proposals of this sort - but in articulating a set of principles that might inform the ongoing debate for left politics anchored both in radical egalitarian democratic values and institutional realism.

New Labour, the market state, and the end of welfare

Jonathan Rutherford

Jonathan Rutherford *looks at the connections between government and the insurance business in their joint project to reduce eligibility for sickness benefits.*

In November 2001 a conference assembled at Woodstock, near Oxford. Its subject was 'Malingering and Illness Deception'. The topic was a familiar one to the insurance industry, but it was now becoming a major political issue as New Labour committed itself to reducing the 2.6 million who were claiming Incapacity Benefit (IB). Amongst the 39 participants was Malcolm Wicks, then Parliamentary Under Secretary of State for Work, and Mansel Aylward, his Chief Medical Officer at the Department of Work and Pensions (DWP). Fraud - which amounts to less than 0.4 per cent of IB claims - was not the issue. The experts and academics present were the theorists and ideologues of welfare to work. What linked many of them together, including Aylward, was their association with the giant US income protection company UnumProvident, represented at the conference by John LoCascio. The goal was the transformation of the welfare system. The cultural meaning of illness would be redefined; growing numbers of claimants would be declared capable of work and 'motivated' into jobs. A new work ethic would transform IB recipients into entrepreneurs helping themselves out of poverty and into self-reliance. Five years later these goals would take a tangible form in New Labour's 2006 Welfare Reform Bill.

Between 1979 and 2005 the numbers of working age individuals claiming IB increased from 0.7m to 2.7m. In 1995, 21 per cent were recorded as having a mental health problem; by 2005 the proportion had risen to 39 per cent, or just under 1 million people. The 2000 Psychiatric Morbidity Survey identified one in six adults as suffering from a mental health problem: of these only 9 per cent were receiving some form of talking therapy. The Health and Safety Executive estimate that 10 million working days are lost each year due to stress, depression and anxiety, the biggest loss occurring in what was once the heartland of New Labour's electoral support, the professional occupations and the public sector. Despite these statistics, Britain has one of the highest work participation rates of OECD countries; while benefit levels are amongst the lowest in Western Europe and benefit claims are on a par with other countries.[1] The system is not in crisis, and this is not the motivation for the proposed changes. New Labour's politics of welfare reform has subordinated concern for the sick and disabled to the creation of a new kind of market state: claimants will become customers exercising their free rational choice, government services will be outsourced to the private sector, and the welfare system will become a new source of revenue, profitability and economic growth.

The road to welfare reform
In 1993 Richard Berthaud of the Policy Studies Institute identified the causes of the continuing rise in IB claimants.[2] In the period of growing unemployment under the Conservative government a fairly constant number of people left work because of ill health, only to find it increasingly difficult to re-enter the labour market. As unemployment began to fall the numbers on IB continued to accumulate. The problem lay not, as the right-wing press insisted, with malingering claimants and collusive GPs, but with the economy and with the hiring and firing practices of

---

1. OECD, *Transforming Disability into Ability - policies to promote work and income security for disabled people*, 2003.
2. See Steven Kennedy, Wendy Wilson, *The Welfare Reform Bill*, Research Paper 06/39, House of Commons Library, 2006; www.parliament.uk/commons/ lib/research/rp2006/ rp06-039.pdf.

employers. Berthaud concluded: 'The increase has not been caused by excessive ease of entry to the system, but by difficulty of exit.' The Conservative government had its own agenda, however, and Peter Lilley, Secretary of State for Social Security in the 1992 administration, pointed the finger at claimants and the way their illnesses were diagnosed by GPs. According to Lilley: 'sickness and invalidity benefits were originally intended for those people who, "by reason of some specific disease or bodily or mental disablement" were unable to undertake work'. Social and psychological causes of illness were now being taken into account and as a result, 'the rules have been progressively widened and complicated'. The definition of incapacity had become 'fuzzy' (quoted in Kennedy & Wilson).

The 1994 Social Security (Incapacity for Work) Act was designed to end the 'fuzziness'. The Act introduced Incapacity Benefit and a number of key reforms to reduce the inflow of new claimants. Lilley hired John LoCascio to advise on 'claims management'. LoCascio was at that time second vice president of Unum, the leading US disability insurance company. He joined the 'medical evaluation group' that was set up to design more stringent medical tests. Another key figure in the group was Mansel Aylward. A new All Work Test was introduced in 1997. Instead of focusing on whether or not an individual was able to do their job, it would assess their general 'capacity to work' through a series of descriptors, for example 'Is unable to cope with changes in daily routine', 'Is frightened to go out alone'. Decisions on eligibility for benefit would be decided by Department of Social Security (DSS) non-medical adjudication officers advised by a newly recruited corps of DSS doctors trained by LoCascio. The new test, and the marginalising of claimants' own doctors, brought the rise in IB claimants to a halt.

Unum's influence was now at the heart of the system of managing disability claims. In April 1997, when the new All Work Test was introduced, the company launched an expensive campaign. One ad ran:

> April 13, unlucky for some. Because tomorrow the new rules on state incapacity benefit announced in the 1993 autumn budget come into effect. Which means that if you fall ill and have to rely on state incapacity benefit, you could be in serious trouble.

LoCascio replied in the negative when *Private Eye* asked if he was not concerned about the conflict of interest involved in his company's advertising campaign, which sought to gain from benefit cuts that he had helped to institute. However Unum Chairman Ward E. Graffam did acknowledge the 'exciting developments' in Britain. Unum's influence in government was helping to boost the private insurance market: 'The impending changes to the State ill-health benefits system will create unique sales opportunities across the entire disability market and we will be launching a concerted effort to harness the potential in these.' [3]

D espite Graffam's upbeat comments, however, the company was in financial difficulties. In the 1980s Unum - along with the two other major life and accident insurance companies, Provident and Paul Revere - had been doing well from providing 'own occupation' income protection schemes for mainly upper income professionals. Insurance against loss of earnings caused by accident or sickness was seen as a lucrative market with strong growth potential. Profit for insurance companies mainly lies in the revenue generated by investing the monthly insurance premiums, and interest rates were high so the companies enjoyed high levels of profitability; they monopolised the sector by sharing a similar disability income policy that offered liberal terms. Two factors threatened future profits however. The first was falling interest rates, and the second was the growth in new kinds of 'subjective illnesses', for which diagnostic tests were disputable. The old industrial injuries were giving way to illnesses with no clear biological markers - Myalgic Encephalomyelitis (ME) or Chronic Fatigue Syndrome (CFS), Fibromyalgia, Chronic Pain, Multiple Sclerosis, Lyme Disease. In the early 1990s the new kinds of claims began to rise just as interest rates fell: profits were threatened. Unum's 1995 'Chronic Fatigue Syndrome Management Plan' sounded the alarm: 'Unum stands to lose millions if we do not move quickly to address this increasing problem'.[4]

It was actually Provident that was quickest off the mark, introducing an aggressive system of 'claims management' that would become the industry norm. It could not influence interest rates, but it could reduce the number of successful claims it paid out. Its Independent Medical Examination (IME) was skewed in

---

3. 'Doctors On Call', *Private Eye*, issue 874, 16 June 1995, p26.
4. My thanks to activists in the US, in particular Linda Nee, and Jim Mooney of corporatecrimefighters.com, who provided me with contacts and information. For the archive of the US campaign against UnumProvident see http://web.archive.org/web/*/http://www.corporatecrimefighters.com

favour of the company through the work undertaken by its claims adjusters and in-house doctors. Illnesses were characterised as 'self-reported' and so thrown into question. Only 'objective' test results were accepted. Some disabling conditions were labelled as 'psychological', which made them ineligible for insurance cover beyond 24 months. Doctors were pressured to use the 'subjective nature' of 'mental' and 'nervous' claims to the company's advantage.[5] Specific illnesses were targeted in order to discredit the legitimacy of claims. The industry drew on the work of two of the Woodstock conference participants, Professor Simon Wessely of King's College and Professor Michael Sharpe of Edinburgh University, in an attempt to reclassify ME/CFS as a psychiatric disorder.[6] Success would allow payouts to be restricted to the 24 month limit for psychological claims and save millions of dollars. By 1997 Provident had restructured its organisation to focus on disability income insurance as its main business. It acquired Paul Revere, and then in 1999 merged with Unum under the name UnumProvident.

That year New Labour introduced the Welfare Reform Act. It was heralded as an answer to Frank Field's call for an end to a culture of welfare dependency, and to Tony Blair's misleading anxieties about levels of spending on social security. All new claimants now had to attend a compulsory work-focused interview. This was partly because the All Work Test introduced by the Tories had failed to reduce the inflow of claimants with mental health disorders. The gateway to benefits therefore needed tightening up. Mansel Aylward, now Chief Medical Officer of the DWP, thus replaced the All Work Test with the Personal Capability Assessment (PCA). The emphasis would no longer be on benefit entitlement but on what a person was able to do and the action needed to support them in work. The task of administering the PCA was contracted out to SchlumbergerSema, which was then taken over (along with its DWP assets) by the US corporation Atos Origin; and in 2005 Atos Origin won a further £500m contract. Claims for benefit were assessed by Atos employees with no medical training, using a computer system called Logical Integrated Medical

---

5. California Department of Insurance Legal Division, 'Accusation', www.insurance. ca.gov/0400-news/0100-press-releases/0080-2005/release089-05.cfm.
6. See the social action research undertaken by M.E. Action UK (www.meaction.org. uk). For example www.meactionuk.org.uk/Notes_on_the_Insurance_issue_in_ME.htm. See also debate in the House of Lords, www.publications.parliament.uk/pa/ld200304/ ldhansrd/vo040122/text/40122-12.htm.

Assessment (LIMA). Unsurprisingly, these computerised evaluations, coupled with clearance time targets for Atos staff, made the PCA unreliable, particularly for those suffering mental health problems. Fifty per cent of IB appeals against the refusal of claims found in favour of the claimant. In 80 per cent of these the problem was poor assessment of mental health problems.[7] While the new Act had succeeded in further restricting the gateway to benefits, it had failed to deliver Blair's promised revolution in welfare. The reform process would go on.

'Active Welfare'

In 2003 the DWP launched its *Pathways to Work* pilot projects. These were forerunners of the kind of 'active welfare' system that had been promoted by UnumProvident and the Woodstock academics. In the pilot projects all new 'customers' to IB undertake a work-focused interview (WFI) with an IB Personal Adviser (IBPA). The Personal Capability Assessments of the 70 per cent who are not screened out by the WFI are fast-tracked, and these claimants (who are deemed not to have severe functional limitations) go on to attend a further series of mandatory, monthly interviews. The role of the IBPAs is to actively encourage customers to consider a return to work, as well as discussing work-focused activity. Customers are offered a 'Choices' package of interventions to support a return to work. For claimants suffering mental illness, a Condition Management Programme is available, developed jointly between Jobcentre Plus and the NHS. A Return to Work credit of £40 per week is payable for twelve months to customers if their new job is not less than sixteen hours, and earns less than £16000. At the Labour Party conference in this same year UnumProvident organised a fringe meeting with employment minister Andrew Smith and health minister Rosie Winterton. Joanne Hindle, corporate services director for UnumProvident, spelt out the future direction of *Pathways to Work*:

Although we can say that we are 90 per cent of the way there in policy terms, the real challenge is delivery - in particular the role of the intermediary. We believe that it is absolutely vital that all employment brokers are properly

---

7. Mind, Welfare Reform Bill 2006 Commons second reading debate Briefing,www. mind.org.uk/.../11D7C4BC-7E8D-438E-A950-96ED5D4469C5/0/ WelfareReformBill2006Mind2Rshortbriefing.pdf.

incentivised to move disabled people along the journey into work and that there are enough of them to do the job. The next step therefore is for private sector to work alongside government to achieve delivery, focus and capacity building within the system.[8]

UnumProvident was building its influence. In 2001 it had launched New Beginnings, a public private partnership that acted as a pressure group, drawing in charities and NGOs and enabling the extension of the company's influence in shaping the policy making environment, particularly in relation to *Pathways to Work*. Its annual symposium had been attended by government ministers, with Woodstock academics providing intellectual input. Then in July 2004, it opened its £1.6m UnumProvident Centre for Psychosocial and Disability Research at Cardiff University. The company appointed Mansel Aylward as Director following his retirement from the DWP in April. Professor Peter Halligan, who had forged the partnership with UnumProvident, was ambitious: 'Within the next five years, the work will hopefully facilitate a significant re-orientation in current medical practice in the UK'.[9] The two men were joined at the centre by Gordon Waddell, an orthopaedic surgeon turned academic and another Woodstock participant. The launch event was attended by Liberal MP Archie Kirkwood, recently appointed Chair of the House of Commons Select Committee on Work and Pensions. Malcolm Wicks, Minister of State in the DWP, gave a speech praising the partnership between industry and the university.[10] UnumProvident could now capitalise on its academic respectability as well as its close government connections. It understood the importance of ideas. Words do not merely describe the world, they enact it. To transform welfare into workfare would involve an ideological battle around language and culture.

Culture of sickness

In 2005 the centre produced a monograph, *The Scientific & Conceptual Basis of Incapacity Benefits* (TSO, 2005), written by Waddell and Aylward and published

---

8. See www.helpisathand.gov.uk/resources/groups/disabilities/ability/ability-magazine-issue-52-november-2003-pdf-825kb.pdf.
9. 'Research Centre Welcomed', 2.7.04, www.cf.ac.uk/psych/cpdr/.
10. Malcolm Wicks, Minister of State for Pensions, www.dwp.gov.uk/aboutus/2004/01_07_04_ucpdr.asp.

by the DWP. In their declarations of interest at the beginning of the text neither man cites their association with UnumProvident. This matters, because the monograph provides the unacknowledged intellectual framework for the 2006 Welfare Reform Bill. And the methodology used by Waddell and Aylward is the same one that informs the work of UnumProvident.

In a memorandum submitted to the House of Commons Select Committee on Work and Pensions, UnumProvident define their method of working: 'Our extended experience … has shown us that the correct model to apply when helping people to return to work is a bio-psychosocial one'.[11] The bio-psychosocial model is explained by Peter Halligan, and Derek Wade of Oxford University (another Woodstock academic), in the *British Medical Journal*: 'The old biomedical model of illness, which has dominated health care for the past century, cannot fully explain many forms of illness.'[12] This old model assumes a causal relation between disease and illness, and fails to take into account how cultural attitudes and psychological and social factors shape illness behaviour. In other words it allows someone to report symptoms of illness, and for society to accept him or her as sick, without their having a pathology. Waddell and Aylward adopt the same argument in their monograph: disease is the only objective, medically diagnosable pathology. Sickness is a temporary phenomenon. Illness is a behaviour - 'all the things people say and do that express and communicate their feelings of being unwell' (p39). The degree of illness behaviour is dependent not upon an underlying pathology but on 'individual attitudes and beliefs', as well as 'the social context and culture in which it occurs'. Halligan and Wade are more explicit: 'Personal choice plays an important part in the genesis or maintenance of illness'.

Waddell and Aylward are exercised by the paradox of a society in which 'objective measures of health are improving' but in which numbers on IB remain 'stubbornly high'. They argue that this can be explained by adopting a bio-psychosocial model. IB trends are a social and cultural phenomenon rather than

---

11. 'UnumProvident Supplementary memorandum submitted by UnumProvident following publication of the Welfare Reform Green Paper', Select Committee on Work and Pensions, see www.publications.parliament.uk/pa/cm200506/cmselect/cmworpen/616/61602.htm.
12. Derick T Wade, Peter W Halligan, 'Do biomedical models of illness make for good healthcare systems?', *BMJ*, Vol.329, Dec. 2004.

a health problem: 'Severe medical conditions only account for about a quarter of the current IB caseload. Most IB recipients now have less severe "common health problems"' (p172). The solution is not to cure the sick, but to transform the culture of welfare and tackle the 'personal and social/occupational factors [that] aggravate and perpetuate incapacity'. Adopting this model will lead to a 'fundamental transformation in the way society deals with sickness and disabilities' (p123). The goal and outcome of treatment is work: 'work itself is therapeutic, aids recovery and is the best form of rehabilitation'. For Waddell and Aylward, work is a virtue. But to make it so, they first abstract it from the material conditions of paid employment. Work becomes an idealised practice shorn of class and inequality and the reality of the large swathes of mundane and boring jobs people must endure. In contrast to their idealisation of work, the authors view worklessness as a serious risk to life. It is 'one of the greatest known risks to public health: the risk is equivalent to smoking 10 packets of cigarettes per day' (p17). No-one who is ill should have a straightforward right to Incapacity Benefit:

> A person who is unwell may 'feel too ill' at present to consider returning to work, but that is not a valid basis for future, permanent incapacity. The argument that, even if they recovered, they could not 'risk' work because it might be 'harmful' to their health is invalid because of the generally beneficial effects of work and the ill effects of long term worklessness (p91).

UnumProvident, in its memorandum to the Select Committee, pursued the same logic, arguing that even the most functionally disabled could be expected to work at some future point.

The Waddell and Aylward monograph draws on the considerable knowledge of the authors, but employs a methodology that skews it towards moral authoritarianism and neo-liberal policy prescriptions. They rely on the much-critiqued and outdated systems theory of sociologist Talcott Parsons, in which the individual and society are assigned to discrete spheres of existence. Hence they acknowledge the social and cultural dimensions of illness, but fail to consider that these and other structural and economic forces might be the dynamic causes of genuine ill health. Instead the *problem* of illness is located in the individual, whose beliefs and behaviour then become the focus of moral judgment and action. As Halligan and Wade argue: 'Our model suggests that illness is a dysfunction of the person in his (or her) physical and social environment'. This follows Parsons's theory of the 'sick role', which he viewed as an individual's deviance from the social norm. He understood society as existing in a state of equilibrium, with individuals functioning in their allotted roles. The sick role upsets this equilibrium because it provides individuals with privileges and exempts them from normal social responsibilities. In order to restore balance society must recognise the sick role as an undesirable state and individuals must accept their moral obligation to recover as quickly as possible and return to work. Waddell and Aylward explain the high levels of IB claimants as arising from a breakdown in this conditionality. The sick role is now assumed to confer a 'right' to incapacity (p47). The solution is to change people's behaviour by transforming the language and culture of welfare, and by using sanctions as a 'motivational tool' to prise people out of their sick role (p166).

UnumProvident exposed

Meanwhile, in the US UnumProvident's business activities had been coming under increasing scrutiny. In 2003, the Insurance Commissioner of the State of California announced that the three big insurance companies had been conducting their business fraudulently. As a matter of ordinary practice and custom they had compelled claimants to either accept less than the amount due under the terms of the policies or resort to litigation. The following year a multistate review identified four areas of concern: an excessive reliance on in-house professionals; unfair construction of doctor's or IME reports; a failure to properly evaluate the totality of the claimants' medical condition; and an inappropriate burden on the claimant to justify eligibility for benefit.[13] UnumProvident was forced to reopen hundreds of thousands of rejected insurance claims. Commissioner John Garamendi described UnumProvident as 'an outlaw company': 'It is a company that for years has operated in an illegal fashion.'[14]

To secure its financial position the company presented a public evaluation of the costs of the multi-state settlement. It estimated that there were potentially 25,000 long-term disability claims (out of a total of 275,000 claimants) that

---

13. 'Targeted Multistate Market Conduct Examination', November 2004, www.maine. gov/pfr/insurance/unum/Unum_Multistate_ExamReport.htm.
14. 'State Fines Insurer, Orders Reforms in Disability Cases', *Los Angeles Times*, 3.10.05, www.insurance.ca.gov/0400-news/0100-press-releases/0080-2005/release089-05.cfm.

would qualify for re-examination. Between $325m and $415m was allocated to cover the likely costs. However this estimate did not include a further potential 14,000 claimants under the separate California settlement. And it was based on a deadline being imposed in early 2007 after which claimants would not be able to elect to have their claim re-examined. The company failed to make it public that this deadline had been nullified by pending multi-district claimants' class actions in Tennessee. This was misleading because there remains the possibility that many more of the 289,000 denied or terminated disability claimants may seek re-evaluation of their claims or litigation. Such potential future actions expose UnumProvident to a potentially ruinous financial outlay.[15]

I n response to the outcry this caused the company has rebranded itself, and has now adopted the name Unum Group. There are reports that as the bad publicity is subsiding the company is returning to its aggressive claims management strategies in order to recover its profitability.[16] In January 2007 a performance rating from Credit Suisse was low, but with an upside driven by higher than expected UK earnings and a lower than expected tax rate.[17] Graffam's strategy has paid off. UnumProvident UK, with 2.3million covered by its insurance schemes and pre-tax profits of £109.8m, provides up to 25 per cent of the post-tax operating income of the UnumProvident group of companies. The company had also played an important role in shaping a workfare culture and policy strategy in the Department of Work and Pensions. In April 2007 UnumProvidentUK changed its name to Unum.

New Labour's Welfare Reform Act

In July 2006 the Government published its second Welfare Reform Bill (which was passed as an Act in May 2007). The aim was to radically reduce levels of worklessness amongst single parents, older citizens and those on Incapacity Benefit (IB), and a target was set of an 80 per cent employment rate amongst working age adults. *Pathways to Work* will be rolled out across the country by 2008. Secretary of State for Work and Pensions John Hutton praised the pilot schemes: 'The largely

---

15. Details received in private correspondence and from Yahoo message boards, http://messages.finance.yahoo.com.
16. Private correspondence; see also, 'Case Reviews fall short for hurt workers', *LA Times*, 12.4.07.
17. www.newratings.com/analyst_news/article_1465881.html.

voluntary approach of *Pathways* has been a success'.[18] But not successful enough. [19] To achieve its target the government will need to reduce the numbers on incapacity benefit by one million, and persuade into work one million more older people, and 300,000 extra lone parents. Employers, particularly in the public sector, will be helped to create more effective management of sickness absence, and benefits will not be given on the basis of a certain disability or illness but on an assessment of the capacity to work. In 2003 the OECD reported that Britain's benefits gateway was 'one of the toughest in the world'.[20] But it was not tough enough, and still more stringent policing was required. The new Act offers GPs and primary care staff rewards for taking active steps to get individuals back into work. 'Employment advisers' will be attached to surgeries to help in 'bringing about a cultural change in the way work is viewed by families and individuals'. The PCA will be redesigned by two technical working groups, one for mental health and one for physical disability. Both groups involve representatives from UnumProvident and Atos Origin.

In 2008, IB will be replaced by a two-tier Employment and Support Allowance. Minister of State for Employment and Welfare Reform Jim Murphy, in a Parliamentary written answer, emphasised that the new allowance will 'focus on how we can help people into work and will not automatically assume that because a person has a specific health condition or disability they are incapable of work'.[21] Apart from those with the most severe disabilities (around 15-20 per cent, who will qualify for a higher rate of benefit) 'customers' who fail to participate in work-focused interviews or to engage in work related activity will be subjected to a 'motivational tool', as suggested by Waddell and Aylward. Current levels of IB average £6500 per annum, but claimants unable to manage or refusing the motivation could lose as much as £10.93 a week, rising to £21.8 for a second refusal of work.[22] There is no evidence to

18. John Hutton, 'The Active Welfare State', speech to the Work Foundation, 16.1.06, www.dwp.gov.uk/aboutus/2006/16_01_06.asp.
19. For statistics and percentages of those entering work through the pathways see David Laws MP written questions to Jim Murphy Minister of State, DWP, 27.3.07, at www.theyworkforyou.com.
20. OECD, op cit.
21. Jim Murphy written answer, www.publications.parliament.uk/pa/cm200506/cmhansrd/cm060620/text/60620w1094.htm.
22. 'Hutton unveils benefits shake-up', BBC news, http://news.bbc.co.uk/1/hi/uk_politics/4641588.stm. Average Benefit rate in Waddell and Aylward, *The Scientific and Conceptual Basis of Incapacity Benefits*, TSO 2005, p85.

suggest that impoverishing people who are ill will prompt them into longer-term employment, and this is particularly true for those with mental health problems. In 2006 the DWP published a report on the impact of the *Pathways to Work* pilots on people with mental health problems. It concluded that: 'the estimated impact of the policy on the outcomes of interest for those who report having a mental illness (as a single health condition) is never statistically different from zero at conventional levels'.[23] The future looks bleak for those who have 'symptoms without diseases', or mental health conditions, and who cannot demonstrate that their illness has an 'objective medical pathology'. Jim Murphy was blunt: 'Work is the only way out of poverty … the benefit system will never pay of itself [enough to lift people out of poverty] and I don't think it should.'[24]

The future of welfare

The Welfare Reform Act is short on detail, and secondary legislation delegates powers to the DWP minister to continue the reform process and tighten up rules. In 2006 Hutton commissioned David Freud, a senior banker at UBS AG, to conduct a review of New Labour's welfare to work policies. Published in March 2007, *Reducing dependency, Increasing opportunity: options for the future of welfare to work* quotes Waddell and Aylward's dictum that work is 'therapeutic' and provides a business model for workfare. Freud argues that the government target can be achieved by bringing in the private sector on long-term, outcome-based contracts. The contracts are central to the success of the scheme. A price per claimant is calculated on the savings in IB costs when the claimant moves back into work. Payments to providers would then be paid over a three-year period from when an individual client enters paid employment. The income generated by the outflow of people from IB would be the incentive driving business towards the government target. The contracting regime would set a minimum standard of service that all 'customers' would receive. However: 'beyond this there would be freedom between the provider and the individual to do what works for them'. Those claimants furthest away from the labour market - and who are most costly

---

23. Stuart Adam et al., *Early quantitative evidence on the impact of the Pathways to Work pilots*, Research Report No 354, DWP 2006.
24. 'Only work ends poverty, says minister', *Financial Times*, 28.3.07.

to the Exchequer - will command the highest rewards.

To carry out this transformation of welfare the DWP would need to establish a new kind of contracting system, which would open up public finance to private companies. According to Freud, the private sector is the only body capable of shouldering the financial risks and arranging the private finance that will reduce costs to the Exchequer. And using the private sector will bring in the banks, which will be able to fund the 'extremely large investments implied here'. Private companies would take the lead in the bidding process for contracts, and in building up consortia of groups in each of the regions and countries in Great Britain. This annual multi-billion pound market, and the creation of regional monopolies, 'would attract major players from around the world' (p62-3). As Freud concludes: 'The fiscal prize is considerable'. Hutton's public reaction was to describe the report as a 'compelling case for future reform'.[25]

Welfare reform exemplifies the transformation of the old style nation state into a new kind of 'enabling' market state. Instead of providing social protection, the market state offers 'opportunities' and 'choice' to 'customers', who in return must shoulder a greater degree of responsibility for their individual predicament. Alongside this transformation in the nature of service provision is the blurring of the boundaries between public service and private business, not least in the revolving door that operates in the higher echelons of the state. The logic of welfare reform is to reduce costs by keeping claims to a minimum. To achieve this, New Labour has adopted the practices of a private insurance company whose claims management in the US has been described as 'illegal'. With the Freud Report it has opened the door for further privatisation.[26] The workfare system that is taking shape in this country is turning the logic of welfare onto its head. It is no longer a system that seeks to help people who are sick or disabled; instead it is increasingly asking them how they can help us. The demand for performativity in return for a meagre subsistence robs people of their autonomy - but New Labour dresses it up in the language of individual career development and dignity for the disabled. John Hutton

---

25. John Hutton, speech on 'Welfare Reform in the UK', 26.3.07, www.dwp.gov.uk/aboutus/2007/26-03.07.asp.
26. Freud's scheme may be a bridge too far for Gordon Brown. See: 'Leak shows that Treasury has consigned Blair welfare privatisation to the back burner', *The Guardian*, 20.4.07,http://society.guardian.co.uk/futureforpublicservices/story/0,,2061933,00.html

describes workfare as a 'something for something' approach, and Tony Blair calls it 'mutual responsibility'. But the compact between the state and an individual whose life has been disrupted by disability or sickness is not an equal one.

The 'sick role' as an explanation for a person's actions and attitudes makes the individual who is incapacitated responsible for what are socially produced problems. The logic of the reforms serves the need of the market, attempting to turn the individual into an efficient, docile unit of consumption and productivity.

The Conservatives have now announced their own approach to welfare reform. Shadow Chancellor George Osborne argues that David Freud has not gone far enough: 'We should seriously consider a bold "no-win, no-fee" approach to getting people off benefits. Prime contractors, be they companies or charities, would be paid primarily if they get people back into work, and keep them there - in other words payment by results.' In return, more will be expected from those on employment related benefits, and tougher sanctions will be introduced against 'those who can work but refuse to take steps to get back into the labour market'.[27] The history of the British welfare system has always been one of grudging, paternalistic and sometimes punitive forms of social protection. But even measured against its own limited ambitions, the future of welfare looks bleak.

---

27. http://www.conservatives.com/tile.do?def=news.story.page&obj_id=137035.

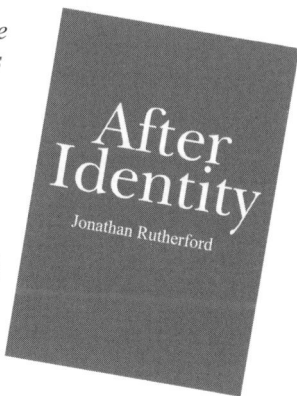

After Identity
Jonathan Rutherford

Once associated with the politics of liberation, identity has since become a more private and individualistic affair: about what we buy and how we look. This book is about rethinking the idea of the individual and ethical life 'after identity'. It addresses these questions in a series of essays – on being an individual; why people fear and hate asylum seekers; memories of England; masculinity and the war on terror; climate change and ecological ethics; and the revolution in ageing.

'There has been thus far no better inventory made of the human consequences of individualisation, and the price which individuals are required to pay for their freedom of self-assertion in a world vacated by the past and denying hospitality to the future. Rutherford has set and furnished the stage on which all debate of the present-day human condition and its prospect will need to be conducted.'
Zygmunt Bauman

'Jonathan Rutherford's consideration of those essential issues – the self, identity – is always thought provoking. Even better, it carries an unusual and heartening optimism.'
Madeleine Bunting

'The problems the thinking left face are complex. Modern consumer capitalism is busily shaping us in its image and destroying the ability to even imagine a different way of being human. Jonathan Rutherford faces up to the complexity of this challenge in a way that is intensely political and immediate.'
Neal Lawson

ISBN 978 1905007 400   160 pages   £17.99

For a post-free copy send cheque to Lawrence and Wishart, PO Box 7701, Latchingdon, Chelmsford, CM3 6WL

Or order from www.lwbooks.co.uk tel: 020 8533 2506 fax: 020 8533 7369 email: orders@lwbooks.co.uk

Democracy and the public realm

Towards a progressive agenda?

Janet Newman and Nick Mahony

*In its deployment of the language of democracy
- devolution, participation, engagement, the 'new
localism' - New Labour has frequently emptied it
of all content. How can we put new life into this
vocabulary, and into democratic practices?*

It is widely argued that we need new thinking about democracy, in order to address widespread disenchantment with the political elite and to fill the vacuum left by greater individuation and the turn to consumerism. But it is important to remember that democracy itself is not an unproblematic good. Democratisation has been part of the US programme for the incorporation of non-western nations into a global project of neo-liberal rule; and it was UK style democracy that took Britain to war against the will of electors, and despite popular attempts to give voice to the public's dissent. This opens up a need not simply for 'more democracy' but for hard thinking about what we mean when we speak of democracy, and about the ways in which a progressive agenda for democratic renewal might be forged. In this article we want to discuss some of the issues involved, and to engage with the arguments in *Democracy and the Public Realm* (edited by Hetan Shah and Sue Goss), the third contribution to the Compass Programme for Renewal. Like the two earlier documents in the series, this draws on a series of conversations in and around the 'progressive' left in Britain, and marks an attempt to carve out a political agenda that is positive and forward looking.

Searching for a progressive politics at this moment in UK history is a project that inevitably has to engage with the failures of New Labour. But it also means confronting its successes - that is, with ideas that have been appropriated and transformed in Labour's own attempt to shape a new political settlement. In what Stuart Hall terms a 'politics of transformism' (in 'New Labour's Double Shuffle', *Soundings* 24), New Labour drew successfully not only on older social democratic strands of politics but also on many other movements (feminism, gay politics, disability movements, anti-racist struggles and others), incorporating and transforming them in its attempt to create a broad mandate for its own particular image of modernity.

The issue here, then, is whether apparently progressive ideas - the devolution of power, greater public participation, innovations designed to engage citizens as active agents in the renewal of the social fabric - can be recaptured from their current dominant framing within the modernising and moralising politics of New Labour. Labour's project seeks to rework these ideas, such that 'devolution' comes to valorise the local, producing a narrowed political imaginary; 'public participation' seeks to harness the public voice as an agent of performance improvement; and 'active citizens' become captured in notions of moralised and responsibilised communities.

In setting out its stall, then, Compass has had not only to present new agendas - for example around the possibilities of transnational democracy - but also to try to detach older agendas from their New Labour incarnations. And here the question of democratic renewal presents particular difficulties, precisely because ideas of devolution, localism, community, public participation in decision-making and democratic innovation pervade Labour's own policy texts (not least the recent White Paper on local government). The very words have been stripped of much of their progressive value - how far can the Compass programme reinvigorate them? And what form of democratic renewal might be possible given the assaults on democratic decision-making that have taken place over the last thirty years and the consequent lowering of trust in and disillusionment with the political system itself?

A further difficulty lies in the different strands of left politics that Compass attempts to reconcile. Democracy, in this document, is cast as an alternative both to 'top-down statism' and to untrammelled market power. This has echoes of a search for a new kind of Third Way, with all of the political tensions that inevitably follow. As Michael Kenny commented in his eloquent response to the first two instalments of the Compass Programme for Renewal,

> The 'grand narrative' of Compass barely masks an important tension in its collective thinking: between, on the one hand, the promoters of the merits of a range of alternative perspectives about 'the good' and, on the other, the age-old ambition of parts of the left to build its moral and political case upon the idea that there is one ultimately superior picture of the good society, which equates with socialism ('Progressive politics after Blair', *Soundings* 35, p102).

It is the 'alternative perspectives' that win the day in *Democracy and the Public Realm*, evident in the reframing of traditional notions of equality and solidarity through the language of democracy. Equality does not disappear from the debates, but is no longer located within a concept of the basic rights of citizenship, instead moving away to a range of sites and practices in which differential access to institutions, services and public goods is debated. This reframing provides some key benefits: first, it insists that we look forwards rather than backwards, taking account of the need to forge lines of solidarity within and beyond the nation state in a globalising world; and second, it opens up democracy itself to critical scrutiny.

The Compass proposals are very wide ranging, covering reform of political institutions, the civil service, local government, the media, trades unions, political parties, the courts, the workplace, the EU, and public services. They include recommendations on the Human Rights Act, ID cards and political lobbying; but also focus on devolution and participation in civil society. There different understandings of democracy at play here, which sometimes are in tension with one another. On one view, power is understood as deeply institutionalised - leading to calls for democratisation through the reform of government, the civil service, the House of Lords, the EU, and so on. A second view understands power as more plural and productive, and searches for an ongoing, 'everyday' democracy of involvement, participation and action. In the comments that follow we focus on the recommendations around the construction of an ongoing, 'everyday' democracy of active citizenship and public participation linked to the devolution of power, not least because we think these themes form the moral and political high ground in current debates.

Public participation

Critics of New Labour have tended to dismiss the emphasis on public participation as 'government by focus group', arguing that initiatives such as the recent Citizens Summit at Downing Street (where 60 'ordinary' citizens were invited to debate the policy programme for the next parliament) are designed to short-circuit, rather than enhance, participative democracy. However the value of deliberative and other forms of participative practice as ways of reviving democratic engagement and steering policy-making should not so easily be dismissed. The Compass Programme provides excellent examples of citizen involvement in decision-making from across the world, and there are many important innovations taking place in the UK. The problem with this is that many of the ideas have been translated into practices that serve, in the end, to reinforce, rather than call to account or even challenge, institutionalised power.[1] This is not a case against innovation - far from it. But it does highlight the need to go beyond a normative vision of participative democracy, whether offered by Compass or others, in order to begin to understand why new forms of participation often fail to realise their potential to create deeper forms of engagement. This means paying attention to the conditions - political, material, institutional and cultural - that both enable and constrain new participatory initiatives.

For example participatory budgeting, one approach to democratic renewal that has had high visibility in recent years, is viewed as a practical means to incentivise and engage citizens in political decision-making. Recognising the radically different forms participatory budgeting has taken in Porto Alegre (Brazil), Modena (Italy) and more recently in a London Borough, we can see the politics of translation in practice. In Porto Alegre the commitment to participatory budgeting was made through an investment in an ongoing process of local engagement, giving citizens responsibility for a proportion of the local municipal budget. Translated to a local London borough context in 2005,

---

1. See for example M. Barnes, J. Newman and H. Sullivan, *Power, Participation and Political Renewal*, Policy Press 2007; and C. Davies, M. Wetherall and E. Barnett, *Citizens at the Wheel*, Policy Press 2007.

participatory budgeting took the form of a one-off event at which a group of local residents were invited to deliberate and vote on a set of pre-defined policy 'options' without any concrete commitment from the council to act on the 'results'. A recent study into this London process demonstrates the range of ways in which the council directed this event, in particular by placing strict limitations on the scope and reach of its outcomes. Deliberations around the issue of waste management, for example, were narrowly channelled by officials into options entailing significant changes to 'consumer' behaviour in the Borough. However some participants responded by suggesting that a tax should instead be levied on companies responsible for the production and distribution of 'excessive' packaging materials. This was a challenge from the margins of a tightly managed event, in which the organisers retained the power to decide whether or not to respond to recommendations and challenges. But this case demonstrates the importance of transcending official constructions of 'local' problems and 'particular' issues, through deliberation about the wider politics that generate them.

Compass constructs for itself the possibility that new political participation processes can be viewed as neutral devices for renewing democracy; but these processes are translated through specific institutional and governmental practices. Whether it is via the advocacy of 'deliberative' practices or of various 'new economy' networked, informal, distributed forms of organisation, there is a tendency to uncritically attribute positive moral qualities to particular forms of organising. Techniques are not politically stable: participatory practices can be used by government in attempts to manipulate or empower; and engaging and 'devolving' responsibility for state services to networks of 'creative' individuals can signal either the break-up or the renewal of such services. Public participation is not an untrammelled good: it lends itself equally well to the focus group of the PR company, to the consumer feedback mechanisms used increasingly by public services, and to deliberative initiatives designed to engage citizens in new forms of democratic decision-making.

This ambiguity is highlighted in another example of a recent public participation experiment. *Vote for Me* was an initiative undertaken by ITV during the lead-up to the 2005 general election. This used a reality TV game-show format in an attempt to engage viewers in a contest to select a prospective parliamentary candidate from a short-list of 'ordinary' members of the British public. Bypassing political parties the programme aimed to facilitate the emergence of an 'authentic' voice of the UK population in the figure of a person that could then go on to stand for election and represent the public's 'real' issues in parliament. Where ITV presumably set out with a rather benign idea of the capacities and political motivations of the British public, viewers - initially encouraged by one of the programmes 'judges' (ex-*Sun* editor Kelvin McKenzie) - eventually selected a 'winner' committed to zero immigration and the castration of paedophiles. Given the emerging consensus around the devolution and participation agenda it will become increasingly important to differentiate between practices that work to popularise political participation and those that generate varieties of reactionary populism.

'Going local'

Devolution and participation appear to form a coherent, and mutually reinforcing, theme that runs throughout the Compass programme, and appear to be quite close to Labour's own vocabulary of reform. This creates both problems and opportunities. It is not surprising that devolution should appear as such a central theme given that the UK is rightly viewed as one of the most centralised governments in the world. It is this centralisation of power - not only towards the executive but also within it - that has progressively impoverished democracy through the Conservative governments of the 1980s and 1990s and successive Labour governments. The Compass report helpfully provides a framework for the reform of Whitehall towards a model that is less likely to hold on to power at the centre. But devolution offers no quick fix. It will be extremely difficult to overcome the years of progressive impoverishment of local government and its consequences: not least the tendency, in some places, for local authorities to attempt to hang on to what little power they retain. As a result many local authorities fail to serve as a good model of democratic practice in their own right, and thus fail to attract new 'entrants' to, or engagement with, the democratic process.

Nevertheless local government has been one source of extensive innovation in terms of devolution to neighbourhoods and attempts to engage the public in forms of collaborative or participative governance at local level. These forms of engagement can be viewed as steps towards what Compass terms a more participative, 'everyday democracy'; and one of the proposals is that public authorities, and local government in particular, should be 'given a duty of public involvement: to engage citizens in helping to set their visions, priorities, targets or budgets, and empower them with the information to do so'. Here Compass discourse is quite close to that of the proposals put forward by proponents of a 'new localism', as promulgated by an influential network of academics and local government leaders, and taken up - in modified form - by David Miliband during his tenure at the Department for Communities and Local Government. If, as Kenny argues, the first two Compass pamphlets were directed towards Gordon Brown as Prime Minister in waiting, the agenda of *Democracy and the Public Realm* feels much more closely aligned to the 'Miliband tendency' within New Labour. Notions of devolution, democracy and community pervade initiatives associated with his Departmental tenure, and - in somewhat watered down form - the 2006 White Paper on local government.

But the emphasis on 'the local' as a privileged site of democratic, participative or collaborative governance has been widely criticised. First, it produces a form of participative politics that limits people (in the form of apparently neatly differentiated 'communities') to local forms of engagement, cutting local constituencies off from the national and global public policy issues that impinge on - and indeed serve to generate - such locales. Second, it conceives of governmental 'centres' and 'local' peripheries as bounded territorial domains. This neither takes on board the myriad ways that contemporary governance is exercised, nor the ways in which communities are configured across, rather than within, different territories. And third, the idea that power is currently 'held' centrally, somehow 'within' central government, is also highly problematic. States don't simply 'have' power; rather they exercise power through their privileged access to resources such as money, technology and expertise, to bring people into various kinds of relationships with processes of governance.[2] Unless they offer citizens greater access to these resources, local participation processes can simply offer governments yet another means through which they can attempt to exercise power over citizens.

Finally, conceiving of locales in this way leads to proposals for new forms of local participatory politics that limit local people to 'locally' focused forms of engagement. Under New Labour such developments have tended to be cast within the rhetoric of community, and the consensual (and often highly moralising or even authoritarian) politics that follow. Thankfully the Compass

---

2. See the work of John Allen, Ash Amin and Doreen Massey.

document avoids this communitarian turn. But the emphasis on the local as a site of progressive democratic practice has the effect of bracketing the wider forms of power that constitute the problems and issues that local people are invited to address; and it also potentially produces a narrowing of the 'political imaginary' that sustains democratic practice.[3]

Sustaining the public realm

The key question that confronts us is how to think the public - and the public realm - not just through, but also beyond, the institutions of the state. This is difficult for many who associate themselves with a state centric social democratic tradition. Compass does a good job of defining the conditions under which the public realm can be sustained (regulation of the market, protection of public assets, greater public involvement and so on, not to mention addressing the role of the media). But ambiguities remain around at least three key issues. The first is how to hang on to a public imaginary in a context in which the limitations of viewing the public as an undifferentiated, universal category have been established. Questions of faith, race and culture cut across notions of publicness in deeply uncomfortable ways. How then might it be possible to forge new constituencies around 'progressive' agendas while at the same time respecting and facilitating the negotiation of differences? Key here is the bridging roles played by those who can 'reach out' to different constituencies while also speaking to power. Crucial bridging roles are played not only by some state workers, but also by community workers, advice centres, advocacy groups and emergent social movements. However, support - especially funding - for such work is highly precarious, and many 'bridging' organisations are themselves being transformed into little more than service delivery units within a contract state.

A second issue is the constitutive power of consumerist discourse. Much has been written about the inroads of consumerism and choice and its effects on the possibility of a collective, public imaginary. Rather less attention has been paid to the ways in which consumerism and choice in public services capture public aspirations and desires and transform them in order to sustain a new phase of modernisation: one in which the public itself is charged with the work of ensuring

---

3. See conclusion to J. Newman, *Remaking governance: peoples, politics and the public sphere,* Policy Press 2005.

that public services adapt to the neo-liberal project. However this constitutive power is not necessarily effective. The literature on the demise of social democracy and the consequent subordination of the public realm to the market, and to neo-liberal logics of rule, offers rather too neat and tidy a story. Work on public service consumerism suggests that the public are not necessarily 'dupes', but can hold different identifications in play as they struggle to reconcile wider public allegiances with more personal interests.[4] There may also be a question of whether the consumerist mode can satisfy the desires that it raises and gives voice to ... and of what happens if it can't; and of how far it might be possible to change the current institutional and political appropriations of consumerism - around, for example, notions of 'ethical' consumption - in order to enable a consumerist ethos to be mobilised for more progressive forms of change.

A third ambiguity is produced by the increasing breakdown of notions of a public domain as it collapses into 'civil society'. Governmental discourse is currently obsessed with the possibilities of civil society as the site in and through which the next phase of the modernisation of the welfare state can be accomplished; as the main source for the renewal of the social fabric; and as offering possibilities for new forms of political engagement that will restore trust in the polity (if not in politicians). Civil society appears here as a space, defined by its 'otherness' to both state and market, and as such can readily be filled by different kinds of politics. This space is therefore imagined in contradictory ways: as empty (of politics) yet full (of values, norms and community belongings). Its promise, then, rests on its apolitical, yet 'authentic' character.

The whole terrain of debate about civil society and its multiple potentialities is so traversed by normative images that the eyes tend to glaze when reading sentences that contain the words, whether in the Compass document or the White Paper. Here the fault line running through this commentary re-emerges: progressive developments - including those that focus on the potentialities of civil society as a source of democratic renewal - can so easily slip and slide into new strategies for governing the social. The focus on civil society in governmental projects may therefore have the effect of closing down the very sources of innovation, dissent and mobilisation from which the next generation

---

4. See J. Clarke et al, *Creating citizen-consumers: changing relationships and identifications*, Sage 2007.

of progressive ideas should flow. We can already trace the way in which civil society organisations are becoming aligned with state and market in new forms of hybrid organisations charged with service delivery, and in the new doctrine of 'social entrepreneurship' as the answer to both unmet social needs and to problems of economic regeneration. These organisational forms, in practice, make it increasingly difficult to discern what is 'public' about public services. And the hegemonic status of discourses of civil society, community and consumerism makes 'speaking the public', and holding a public identification that can sustain public action, increasingly difficult (see Janet Newman, 'A Politics of the Public', *Soundings* 32).

Conclusion

Compass's attempt to engage a wide range of people and groups in debates about democracy and the public realm is very welcome. The process through which this document was developed offers its own template for democratic political practice - a template incorporating open deliberation, both face to face and through the internet; wide engagement; and clear connections to wider networks. Its inclusive approach avoids any static notions of representation. This was, then, an iterative process of dialogue without premature closure; an enabling, consensus building and facilitative process that enabled the mutual accountability of those involved. This of course makes critiques problematic: those with an interest in the topics discussed here had ample opportunities to participate in the online debates and to comment on a series of drafts.

But at some point the process has to deliver a product: political debate has to result in public action. And it is here that the difficulties of alternative, open and deliberative forms of engagement become clear. Michael Kenny commented on the problems of producing programmatic statements - that they are redolent of 'old style' party politics, in which the manifesto forms a platform through which electors are persuaded to support a party or its leader. But it is hard to discern who it is that is to be persuaded by the Compass Programme for Renewal (other, perhaps, than Gordon Brown - but this is surely too limiting a conception of the political intent of Compass). And the dissemination of a series of programmatic statements about what should happen next tends to close debate down - all one can do is agree or disagree. The Compass Programme has to be viewed, then, as a sounding board and stimulus for wider engagement and debate beyond, as well as within, the left-of-centre enclaves offered by think-tanks, parties and journals. Even if the answers are sometimes troubling, the questions raised by Compass are precisely those that need to inform debate as New Labour begins - perhaps - to lose its stranglehold on political discourse.

This nevertheless begs the question of how such public debates should be continued in a context in which there has been a collapse of faith in the institutions of state, political parties and political representatives. Part of the challenge will be to think about how it might be possible to develop programmes for the 'good' society not just within such institutions but in collaboration with plural publics 'outside' them. The success of contemporary pressure groups and the mobilising politics of European and World Social Forums, anti-globalisation movements and other struggles can be linked to the ways in which they tap into the passions and enthusiasms of new constituencies, using the media, the internet and public events. With such informal modes of political activism becoming increasingly important, however, questions are raised about how the affective registers in which they may be conducted can be mediated and connected to more formal political processes. This not only raises questions of political style and problems of representation; it also opens up the potential of collapsing both social diversity and transnational affiliations into a flattened plain of national politics.

This is where the mediating work of Compass and other groups - professionals, voluntary organisations, community groups, local partnership bodies and even political parties - becomes so significant. If successful, it offers the potential to open up new spaces in the political system in which alternative agendas can emerge. Hopefully these might offer more complex ideas and practices of 'community', and richer and more expansive understandings of the 'local' and 'particular' as produced through wider dynamics of territory and scale. The challenge, however, is to prevent new and imaginative ideas - such as those offered by Compass - from being incorporated into the political system in ways that strip them of their radical potential for renewal. The politics of transformism - ideological, institutional and governmental - are perhaps the terrain on which the centre or progressive left, and of the social movements and local struggles that inform and renew it, must be fought.

What's wrong with happiness?

Michael Rustin

Michael Rustin argues that greater well-being is unlikely to be promoted in a system whose main goal is increased economic efficiency.

This article is a contribution to the debate on the questionable connections between economic growth and enhanced happiness among populations in already-affluent societies.[1] I will first review current discussion of these questions - debate about which arises in part from the existence of separate measures of public happiness and income levels. I will then discuss whether increased 'happiness', with its philosophical origins in utilitarianism, is the best way of framing the idea of the good for individuals and societies - suggesting that it is at any rate insufficient for this purpose. Finally, I will focus on the way in which Richard Layard has framed these questions, and in particular on the way in which he addresses the problems of mental health in this context, by means of his proposal for a large-scale programme of cognitive behaviour therapy.

---

1. In societies which have not yet escaped from mass poverty, economic growth and well-being *are* closely connected. For more on these debates see, for example, L. Bruni and P.L. Porta (eds), *Economics and Happiness*, Oxford University Press 2005; Oliver James, *Affluenza*, Vermilion 2007; Robert E. Lane, *The Loss of Happiness in Market Democracies*, Yale University Press 2000; Richard Layard, *Happiness: Lessons from a New Science*, Penguin 2005; Avner Offer, *The Challenge of Affluence: Self-Control and Well-Being in the United States and Britain since 1950*, Oxford University Press 2006; *The Economist*, 'Happiness and how to measure it', 23.12.06-5.1.07.

Happiness and wealth

Societies like ours are getting richer, but are they getting any happier? This is now becoming a major topic of debate, with a growing literature. It is argued that the connection long assumed to exist between increased affluence and happiness or 'subjective well-being' is actually weak for countries above a fairly basic level of prosperity - defined at an annual average gross national product of around $15,000 or $20,000 dollars per head of population. Since many governments in rich countries make continuing economic growth their primary political goal, the evidence that this does not lead to improvements in people's well-being is, or should be, a serious matter for public policy.

There have been many studies of self-reported happiness, or subjective well being, in different countries, from 1950 onward; and nation-by-nation comparisons show only a small correlation between income levels and self-reported well-being, once countries reach the GNP level mentioned above. Countries where average per capita income is between $20,000 and $35,000 have satisfaction rates only a few percentage points above a whole range of countries where income is below $10,000 (see Richard Layard, *Happiness*, p32). Though the lowest satisfaction rates are in the poorer countries, a number of nations where average income is under $10,000 have average happiness levels close to those of much richer countries.

Furthermore, in the period in which the latter has been systematically measured, improvements in living standards in nations such as the United States and Britain are associated with no improvement - indeed slight decline - in subjective well-being. One US study found that between 1972 and 1994, a time when income increased massively, the percentage of the population reporting themselves to be 'very happy' fell by four percentage points (from just over 34% to just over 30% - see Robert Lane's *The Loss of Happiness*, p20). Generally, in the United States, self-reported happiness has declined in the postwar period. The rich invariably report themselves in surveys to be happier than the poor (just as they enjoy better health and longer life-expectancy). But their self-reported degree of happiness does not increase over time even though their absolute level of wealth has greatly increased over the past decades (see *Happiness*, p30; *The Loss of Happiness*, p5).

Other kinds of evidence support these findings. Crime levels greatly increased during the period of the most rapid rise in prosperity (and, counter-intuitively, of full employment too, which one might have expected to reduce crime levels). Family breakdown, measured in divorce rates and the incidence of single-parent families, also increased markedly, though there has been some stabilisation in both in the last decade or so. Mental illness has increased, to the point that Richard Layard has identified it as one of the major problems facing governments. All does not seem to be well.[2] Why not?

Defining the problem

Why might there be a weak or even inverse relationship between economic growth and happiness? One reason is what is called the adaptation effect Improvements in living standards - higher income, more goods and services, more travel - lead us continually to upgrade our view of what we need. The satisfaction we gain from our large television set is eroded by the appearance of high definition television; in our new car by the superior models that every year come on to the market. We find ourselves on what is described as an *hedonic treadmill*, which keeps us working and accumulating, but only in order to stay in the same place as far as our actual satisfaction is concerned.

A second reason emerges from critiques of the assumptions of the neo-classical economic paradigm that has been so influential in shaping our modern economic system. The idea here is that increased wealth has diminishing marginal utility, in relation to other goods that have to be foregone in order to achieve it. Any good, in economic theory, becomes relatively less valuable, relative to other goods, as it becomes more abundant. An additional unit of wealth in an affluent society will thus be experienced as of less value than the goods that have to be foregone to obtain it. If rising incomes are achieved only at the cost of - in Robert Lane's terms - less companionship, or less time spent with our children, partners or friends, or doing the things that we most enjoy, then it is no surprise if we do not feel happier for being richer, and perhaps less happy.

---

2. Data is provided by Layard (in *Happiness*) and Offer (*The Challenge of Affluence*). For example, crime levels increased threefold in the period from 1950 to 1980, though the increase has now levelled off. Half of all American children are living with only one parent by the age of 14. Three times more young people received psychotropic medication in 1997 than in 1987; anxiety scores among children have increased such that the average child of the 1990s would in the 1950s have been deemed in need of professional attention.

A third reason, set out by Richard Layard in his book *Happiness*, concerns rivalry, or what sociologists used to call 'relative deprivation'. We measure our well-being not only by reference to our own past situation, but also by the situation of others, within our reference group. If other people have more, we feel that we have less. The sense of improvement or otherwise is relative, so if we are no better off relative to others, we may feel no improvement in our well-being even if our absolute purchasing power increases. (Experiments testing people's attitudes to hypothetical changes in their own and others' income have shown that people's sense of well-being is lessened by imagining that others are doing better, even if their own absolute situation is unchanged.) I remember when I used to have management responsibility for a Faculty in a university, recognising that the opportunity that the university sometimes gave for staff to compete for promotion would very likely be the source of misery rather than pleasure, since more people would end up unpromoted than promoted, and rivalries would be increased by the competition.

Degrees of inequality also influence subjective well-being. Country-by-country comparisons show that more equal societies, such as the Scandinavian countries, have higher levels of reported happiness than more unequal ones, such as the United States or Britain. This finding adds to what has previously been established in the sphere of health and illness (where Richard Wilkinson has found that more equal societies are on average healthier, and that the steeper the hierarchy of distribution of income and wealth, the worse the average health of those occupying inferior positions). Country-by-country comparisons also show a lower incidence of 'social diseases', such as crime and addiction, within more equal societies. This may be a consequence of the fact that in maintaining a more equal distribution of wealth and income, those societies are manifesting respect and concern for all, especially the less well-off, as well as of the fact that a sufficiency of goods and services (health care, education and housing for all, for example) gives rise to greater aggregate satisfaction than would a greater abundance of goods available to the rich alone.

Critics of economic growth as the overriding objective of governments argue that it produces disbenefits that outweigh its material gains. Thus, if geographical mobility increases, job security is reduced, and social solidarity, especially in the form of family ties, grows weaker; people will then lose more than they gain from higher income - in 'goods' that *they* value but which are undervalued by the market. If subjective well-being, as Robert E Lane argues, is enhanced most by feelings of being respected and accorded recognition, then social processes which undermine these conditions will make us feel worse, even if we have a larger salary to spend each year.

There is a further paradox. The equation of the true wealth of a community with the economic statistics which measure this wealth, is misleading. A great deal of 'value' (in terms of what gives satisfaction) is generated outside the sphere of market exchange. The 'goods' generated by many activities within the home (cooking meals, playing with the children, having a conversation, entertaining friends) are invisible in the national accounts, except to the degree that they entail expenditures to sustain them. It has been calculated (though estimates of this differ) that national income as it is measured in the market sphere accounts for less than half of true 'national wealth', if one also assigns a notional monetary value to non-marketised activities.

Parents who stay at home two days a week to look after their young children, instead of doing paid work, are reducing their own and the 'national income' by so doing, even if the benefit to them and the children is greater than that which would be brought by two days' extra earnings. In the terms of the money economy they will be poorer, but in terms of their psychic, relational and social economy, they may be richer, and their children even more so.

Robert Lane points to another mismatch between measures of welfare generated by the market and actual benefit, within the sphere of paid work itself. In neo-classical economic theory, work is seen as something whose disbenefits have to be compensated by wages and salaries. (In

'a sufficiency of goods and services gives rise to greater aggregate satisfaction than would a greater abundance of goods available to the rich alone'

another words it is treated as a cost, not a benefit; its value is measured solely by the payments made in return for it.) This ignores the intrinsic benefits which arise from work itself, from the enjoyment of human faculties, from its sense of achievement, and from the relations with others which it involves. These benefits go unmeasured in calculations of Gross National Product. It is thus quite possible that the marketable wealth that may be generated by some 'efficiency gains' in work practices may be more than offset by the losses to well-being in the activity of work itself. Some intrinsic goods in the experience of consumption are also undervalued by the market. Thus people may enjoy better value from lower prices when they shop at out-of-town supermarkets, but lose value from the friendly contact they formerly enjoyed with local shopkeepers and neighbours, or from the decline of the quality of the urban environment. Such losses of well-being are more severe for those who do not have resources to make use of more distant shopping places.

The continuing increases in national wealth of recent years have been achieved in part through the expansion of the sphere of monetised exchange (though technological and organisational advances are also factors). More ready-prepared meals are bought and consumed; more people eat out, there are more families in which both parents take paid work, more caring of various kinds is done by paid staff. Gift-exchange, which Karl Polanyi thought central to pre-capitalist economies, is diminished, especially within Britain and the USA, while market exchange expands.[3] And we 'import' migrants from other countries, to sustain our own 'economic growth'. (For the migrants themselves, the shift from a world of informal or gift exchange to marketised relationships is even more marked.[4])

These factors help us to understand why there may be a negative rather than positive correlation between the gradient of rising material wealth and that of subjective well-being. The emergence of doubts of this kind in public debate may now be starting to have political resonance. Also relevant to these doubts about the benefits of increased wealth are anxieties about climate change, and the wider problems of resource scarcity that are likely to come from the further industrialisation of countries such as China and India. The lifting-out of poverty of millions of people is wholly to be welcomed, but as large sections of these populations begin to aspire to the same levels of consumption as Americans and Europeans, it is indeed high time that we asked some questions about the

---

3. Karl Polanyi, *The Great Transformation*, Beacon Press 1944.
4. Arlie Russell Hochschild (in B. Ehrenreich and A. Hochschild (eds), *Global Woman: Nannies, Maids and Sex-Workers in the New Economy*, Granta 2002) has written eloquently about the global economy of child care, in which women from poor countries like the Philippines go to rich countries like the US to care for the children of American working parents, whilst their own children are cared for at home by grandparents. An income stream is repatriated back home, but the core process is the removal of women from the sphere of non-monetary work with their own children, which is thereby depleted, to take part in a marketised exchange in the rich world. One can see why these choices get made, on all sides, but if inequalities were less, the Philippino women would stay at home with their own children.

desirability and sustainability of giving priority to economic growth in the nations of the west that are already rich.

What drives this system?

Since many people feel overstressed by the demands of the market economy, and to a degree recognise the unhappiness to which it gives rise, it is a problem to understand why its dynamic seems so irresistible. Why do governments give such priority to 'economic growth', and take such pride in its achievement, when it seems clear that its benefits in an improved 'quality of life' are so limited? What are the primary drivers of a system that gives such priority to the accumulation of wealth?

One should first note that most people are employed by hierarchical organisations, in which in return for the opportunity to work, receive pay and maybe some economic security, they are required to do as they told. This is the case whether organisations are private or public. So if organisations are driven by the will to make profits, or to balance their budgets, it will be difficult for their members to give priority to other goods, except informally, or in such space as an organisation decides to concede to them. Organisations in the market sector are driven by the necessity to make profits, and those who own their capital, and their senior managers, are dedicated to these purposes. It seems likely that the CEOs of large companies are not motivated so much by the desire to enhance their capacity to spend or to consume more, but rather by their 'competitive instincts' - their desire to succeed, have high status in their own social world and to exercise power (their income and wealth are so substantial, and their leisure is so constrained, that consumption can hardly be the primary goal for them). As Schumpeter well understood, a capitalist system is driven by entrepreneurs with strong wills and competitive drives.[5]

Public bureaucracies have in the past been less single-minded in their goals than organisations operating in the market. They have often given more scope than market-based organisations to other values. This has often been seen as rendering public sector organisations less 'efficient' - in terms of the cost of the goods and services they provide - than those operating in the market, and this has been a justification for privatisation and for creating 'internal markets'

---

5. J. Schumpeter, *Capitalism Socialism and Democracy*, Allen and Unwin 1943.

within them. But accompanying this greater economic 'efficiency' has been more single-mindedness, a determined privileging of the goal of cost-effectiveness over competing values. This is seen as giving priority to the needs of consumers, over those of producers, and is reflected in pressures on the workforce, which often reduce their autonomy or job security. They may be encouraged to concentrate not on their own conception of a 'job well done', but on making sure that the 'cost-centre' to which they are attached meets its financial targets.

There are plainly some benefits to be derived from giving priority to consumers over producers (though with the qualifications that most citizens are employees as well as consumers, and that the 'goods' of lower prices and greater consumer choice may be accompanied by 'bads' such as the experience of reduced security in their workplace). But a single-minded concentration on economic efficiency does not always necessarily benefit consumers - for example where the pleasures of consumption include relationships with providers which become attenuated in the pursuit of efficiency. The 'impersonalisation' of the provision of goods and services is a widespread phenomenon, as anyone who phones a call-centre well knows. Thus many employed individuals are compelled by their conditions of employment to give their priority to income-maximising goals, for their employers, at the expense of other values.

A second important driver of the priority given to market values - at individual, organisational and governmental levels - is economic anxiety. It is not just that profitability and economic growth are deemed good in themselves, but there is fear that if a company, institution or nation falls behind in the competitive race, harmful consequences will necessarily follow. Global competition, as our government never ceases to remind us, is a serious worry. One might imagine that if one settled for less than our 'trend rate' of economic growth, we could then give more priority to different goals, such as greater security, a more equal society, more fulfilling work, a more participatory public life, more creative leisure. But in fact any 'slackening off' of economic competitiveness is feared to bring the risk of real economic decline, which could then bring unemployment, impoverishment and social resentment. While improvements in material standards may bring little apparent improvement in happiness, there does seem reason to fear that a significant deterioration in these *would* have damaging social consequences.

Our government in Britain is in any case committed to 'enrichment' as a good in itself, and has conspicuously allied itself to those its leaders deem to be the major 'wealth creators' in society. But it is also motivated by these anxieties about competitiveness, theorised for it by sociologists such as Anthony Giddens in the ideas of 'globalisation' and the 'risk society'. Thus the education system is remodelled to enhance standards of performance (rather than the happiness and creativity of children) in order that those leaving school will be more employable. Economic efficiency is defined as the overriding objective of public sector organisations (such as NHS Trusts or universities), even at the expense of their primary purposes, on grounds that continued national economic competitiveness depends on it. Of course there are good reasons for deploying scarce human resources for the greatest benefit, but the measures used to effect these equations are often perverse in their effects. For example, it may be more 'efficient' to have no university class with less than fifteen students in it, but there is will usually be a loss of intensity and quality of learning in groups as large as this.

The idea that a capitalist economy forces all those within its power to compete to the utmost, not because they necessarily wish to do so, but because they risk being destroyed by their competitors if they don't, was formulated by Marx, for example in his 1848 pamphlet *Wage Labour and Capital.*[6] This imperative has always coexisted with other values in society - for example the economy of gift exchange within families - but in the present era of a dominant global capitalist economy, this economic pressure on everyone is greater than ever, on nearly everyone.[7]

The consequence is that although one can see that individual and social well-being are (in industrially developed countries) by no means closely correlated with rates of economic growth, there are great difficulties in de-coupling these two definitions of the good. The major institutions which control economic

---

6. 'We see how in this way the mode of production and the means of production are continually transformed, revolutionised, how the division of labour is necessarily followed by still greater division of labour, the application of machinery by still greater application of machinery, work on a large scale by work on a still larger scale. That is the law which again and again throws bourgeois production out of its old course and which compels capital to intensify the productive forces of labour, *because* it has intensified them, it, the law which gives capital no rest and continually whispers in its ear, go on, go on...', *Wage Labour and Capital*, Chapter 5.

7. Marx's prognoses for a communist future, and his political conception of how to arrive at it, had many limitations, his analysis of the expansive and transformative power of capitalism was remarkably prescient. On this argument, see Meghnad Desai, *Marx's Revenge: The Resurgence of Capitalism and the Death of Statist Socialism*, Verso 2002.

resources, and which employ most citizens, are designed and legally sanctioned to pursue profit above all other purposes. These organisations also shape a system of mass communications that systemically defines the good in terms what can be purchased and consumed in the market-place, for their own advantage.[8]

Avner Offer's fine book, *The Challenge of Affluence* (see note 1) adds further dimensions to this analysis. He identifies an increasing disequilibrium since the 1950s between people's aspirations, continually over-stimulated within an individualist consumer society, and their actual satisfaction. He sees the consequence to be a prevailing 'short-termism' of choices, taken without understanding of longer-term costs, and in particular of costs to others. The epidemics of obesity and addiction are one symptom of this - the consequence of the dislocation of consumption from the social relationships which give it meaning. The decline of family solidarity, and the increasing numbers of individuals experiencing divorce or separation, and of children thereby deprived of the care of two parents, is another instance. Offer argues that the advertising industry contributes not only to this climate of hyper-stimulation, but also to a deeper debasement of the media of public communication. He describes a kind of contamination of the sacred, in the way in which audiences are continually invited to believe in, and be moved by, images and persons which they know to be fundamentally dishonest. Social trust is thereby diminished. This argument is an eloquent restatement of Durkheim's sociological critique of anomic and egoistic forms of solidarity, in which the necessary social and moral containment of human aspirations and desires is made weak.

Another dimension of this argument is set out in Stefano Zamagni's essay on happiness and individualism in *Economics and Happiness* (see note 1 for details). Zamagni argues that the neo-classical economic paradigm of interest-maximising individuals has made it impossible to see that most satisfactions are found in contexts of relationship, such that an individual's well-being cannot be separated from the well-being of those to whom they are relationally connected. For example, the well-being of parents is connected to the well-being of children, of teachers to that of their pupils, of artists to the audiences who enjoy what they create. The necessary *social* dimensions of well-

---

8. My argument here gives more emphasis to the institutional power of capitalism and its institutions than most of the writers I cite, who tend to focus their explanations on unintended consequences, external diseconomies, and misguided or myopic motivations.

being, and their location in different possible ways of life, are neglected by models which privilege individual satisfactions and the economic transactions by which these are supposed to be secured.

Governments usually do represent intrinsic claims of value, as well as those signified by the exchange values of the market. This is partly through their historical embodiment of societal goods (e.g. those signified by 'the nation' or aspects of its heritage), and partly because they are elected to give effect to collective social purposes, such as greater social justice. But while our governments do give effect to such social choices through law and taxation, and through mostly feeble attempts to articulate some vision of social possibility, they have in recent decades chosen to make economic growth their overriding commitment. No-one in government seems to feel at this point that it is politically safe to ask whether this priority should become something to be openly debated rather than taken for granted.

Current doubts about the validity of economic growth as a measure of well-being have a history. In the 1970s Amartya Sen was influential in his critique of the global outcomes of market-led economic policies, and measures of economic improvement were instituted that were different from those of GNP or GNP per capita. The Human Development Index produced each year by the United Nations has been one valuable outcome of this critique. This sets out indices of well-being, including such dimensions as infant mortality, mortality and fertility rates, clean water supply and sanitation, education (not least for girls) - which give measures of improvement more discriminating, egalitarian and public-spirited than crude GNP calculations. These ways of thinking have had some considerable influence, including on the British government.

Domestically, the UK government attempts to measure social improvement by social indicators of these kinds. The public sector culture of targets and indicators in part reflects the idea that specific measures of well-being (health or educational outcomes for example) can be given genuine substance, and can stand with the rate of economic growth as a criterion of governmental and national success. However, such measures have often been diverted in their effects by being used as proxies for market indicators, instead of as substitutes for or alternatives to them, and as coercive instruments of marketisation. Levels of 'educational performance', or 'health performance' can be defined as the measures of quality of a *product*, to be chosen in competition by consumers just like any other product in the market place. These measurements of output are thus utilised not to help achieve acceptable standards for all, but for the manufacture of a quasi-market, in which both producers and consumers must compete with one another in their own self-interest. There is present somewhere in this frame the common goal of ensuring that absolute standards *are* raised by these indicators, and an acknowledgement of the relevance of social goals (literacy, health etc) of some kinds. And in a governmental climate which was more genuinely democratic and pluralist in its capacity to sustain a debate about social priorities, indicators of well-being of these kinds could become resources for making genuine public choices. However, in the last ten years they have become the means by which governments impose the disciplines of competitive markets on both the providers and users of public services.

The debate about economic growth and happiness has allowed more attention to be given to questions about what should be the objectives of government - and the goals of society - in addition to, or other than, the pursuit of 'economic growth'. It also suggests that we should be exploring the consequences, both positive and negative, of settling for a desired rate of economic growth that is deliberately lower than the maximum feasible, in order to make space for other social goods.[9]

The idea of happiness

Among the most influential critiques of the equation of rising income levels with improved well-being have been economists (like Amartya Sen) and philosophers (like Martha Nussbaum) who have rejected the utilitarian concept of 'the greatest happiness of the greatest number' as an adequate criterion of the social good.[10] They have argued that the idea of a single measure of welfare, equated with the satisfaction of desires or preferences, does not adequately recognise the diversity of human ends, and the need for freedom to deliberate and decide between

---

9. One of the traps inherent in the choice of economic growth as a summative goal is to see it as the precondition of all other goals. Thus, if we have greater wealth we can then decide whether to spend it in this or that way. But this neglects the reality that the pursuit of economic growth involves the sacrifice of other goals in its pursuit, and in any case tends to genuine mentalities in which 'private' goods are seen as entitlements, and public ones merely as entailing losses, rather than gains, in private benefit.
10. See Amartya Sen, *Development and Freedom*, Oxford University Press 1999; Martha Nussbaum, *Upheavals of Thought*, Cambridge University Press 2001.

them. They have instead defended an Aristotelian conception of happiness as, in Nussbaum's term, 'human flourishing', or in Amartya Sen's, the development of human capacities, as providing a more illuminating language for the framing of human ends.

These critics of utilitarianism believe that the neo-classical economists' equation of preferences and the 'utility' they signify with the happiness of subjects is too one-dimensional and simplistic to provide the language of social choices that is needed. While fully accepting the necessity for markets to allocate goods and resources, Sen has insisted that democratic deliberation and the power of governments are also essential to secure well-being and give effect to people's preferences.[11] Among the arguments against the equation of happiness with utility are the problems that a hedonistic theory of motivation faces in giving attention to the well-being of others, and the fact that deliberation on what we *should* desire is just as important to a good society as the satisfaction of whatever desires we may have already been habituated to feel by circumstances.

Essays published in Amartya Sen and Bernard Williams' collection *Utilitarianism and Beyond* developed this critique more than twenty years ago.[12] For example, in his contribution Stuart Hampshire argued that, while 'stripped-down' concepts of the good - like the 'greatest happiness of the greatest number', or prescriptions of just and moral actions that conform to universalist norms - were valid for the universalist sphere of ethics, they were inadequate to spheres of life which were necessarily more culturally specific. He argued that people were unavoidably born 'into both a natural order and a cultural order' ... 'sexuality, old age, death, family and friendship are among the natural phenomena which have to be moralised by conventions and customs, within one culture or another, and that means within a very particular and specific set of moral requirements' (p156). The problem with equating all judgements with the criterion of utility is that self-interest becomes the primary ground of all choices, with the social consequences for our form of life that we have been describing. Charles Taylor,

---

11. Sen holds that the conjunction of markets to organise distribution, with a democratic political framework, has been the most effective means of alleviating famines where these have occurred, India since Independence having been more successful in this respect than it was before under the Raj, or than China has been within the same period.
12. Amartya Sen and Bernard Williams (eds), *Utilitarianism and Beyond*, Cambridge University Press 1982.

in the same collection, argues that the language of utility is in itself limited, since it takes out of the field of consideration choices that moral agents need to make about specific and not necessarily compatible virtues. The 'qualitative' questions about what it is to be a good soldier, scientist, therapist, friend or parent, and the language in which we try to answer such questions, are as relevant to ethics as the 'quantitative' norm that all should be considered as having an equal moral claim. Taylor's view of a good society requires that we be able to reflect on and make choices about, the range of goods to which people can aspire, and their relation to each other. Ethical perspectives of a 'social' kind, which attach importance to relationships, respect, recognition, and creativity as key elements of a good society, are likely to find this neo-Aristotelian conception of 'happiness as human flourishing' more congenial than the utilitarian idea of the maximisation of satisfactions.

There seem to be considerable difficulties in supplanting the one-dimensional goal of economic growth and rising incomes with more multi-dimensional conceptions of well-being. These difficulties have two main sources. One arises from the norms of our economic system, within which it seems compelling to equate greater purchasing power with more choice and opportunity for individuals. (The 'external diseconomies' and unintended consequences that might undermine the value of such choices are not always easily recognised, as we have seen.) Even when the importance of public goods, requiring collective decisions, is fully recognised, the assumption is understandably made that if gross national product were higher, there would then be more disposable resources to devote to such goods: there may seem to be no contradiction between the goal of greater economic growth, and the advancement of other social goods.[13] The default position of our individualised and marketised system is that private goods should come first, while public and social goods follow only as a derogation from them. It is not recognised that this assumption embodies a choice of values too.

The second problem derives from our highly centralised political system. Parties and governments are obliged by the necessity to win electoral support to

---

13. Social democrats like Anthony Crosland thought that economic growth was the key to the advancement of socialist goals like greater quality and more public goods, since it would be much easier to find resources for such goods from economic surpluses than from redistribution of existing income and wealth.

formulate clear and intelligible objectives and policies which will further them. Complex goals and goods are unavoidably simplified and aggregated in this process. The achievement of an acceptable rate of economic growth in these circumstances is a compellingly simple criterion of governmental success. There is simply not much space, in a centralised system of government, in which the populace is in fact empowered to make few effective choices, for the diversification of goals and political negotiation about them. Furthermore, governments and politicians in a highly centralised system seem to be overwhelmed by complexity, and to need to simplify in order to retain the semblance of control. Society, in the information theorists' language, has a greater 'variety' than the political system that has to govern and regulate it. If we want a greater diversity of goods to be recognised and furthered, we will need a greater diversity of deliberative settings in which goals can be formulated and contested. In other words, if we want to see a more differentiated vocabulary of public goods and choices, we need a more devolved and participatory political system. In this respect, small *is* beautiful.

Richard Layard's programme for mental health

Richard Layard has been making use of Benthamite philosophical ideas - of which he is an avowed admirer - to advocate a more socially responsible public policy. He argues that it is not only analysis of external diseconomies and the unintended consequences of economic behaviour that argue the need for major interventions in market arrangements; scientific measures, including empirical studies of people's reports of their own happiness, and neuroscientific studies of its correlates of happiness in brain-function also lend support to this view.[14] Layard defends giving priority to public goods, and to greater equality and job security through the tax system; and he prefers the Continental European model of higher taxation, greater equality, and more universal social entitlement, to the free market model of the USA. He is a committed, if moderate, social democrat, and has been an effective advocate of full employment policies. In his book he advocates a considerable range of governmental interventions (for example welfare-to-work, compulsory parenting classes, and a considerable expansion in mental health services) to advance the general happiness - of the kind to which

---

14. He has a discussion of the location of positive emotions in the right forebrain, and negative emotions in the left, which seems extraordinarily simplistic.

the present government, to which Layard has been an adviser, has shown some commitment.

Given that Layard questions the links between economic growth and the general happiness, and seems to be willing to trade a slower rate of growth for qualitative benefits in well-being, does this argument about philosophical frameworks really matter? Is there anything wrong with 'happiness', as defined by utilitarians, or not?

Layard's philosophical assumptions do make some difficulties for his argument. He is an advocate, like Bentham, of universalism, of the principle of the greatest happiness of the greatest number, rightly pointing out that the great virtue of this principle is that it assigns equal moral weight to all individuals. But it is one thing to assert this as a universal moral principle, another to explain why individuals might choose to care about the well-being of others as much as they care about their own. Layard's efforts to reconcile the motivational principle of self-interest, basic to liberal economic theory, with the principle of altruism which he ethically prefers, are not convincing. He explains the greed and short-sightedness regarding interests displayed by citizens in our market society as an evolutionary hangover from hunter-gatherer times when, in Hobbes's terms, life was 'nasty, brutish and short'. He says there is no reason why we should remain 'enslaved' by this genetic inheritance. But if selfishness really is our genetic inheritance (which it isn't in this simple way), modifying human behaviour is going to be more of a problem than Layard supposes.

Indeed evolving a shared conception of the common good is a generic problem for societies based on market principles. This is a central issue which the debate about 'happiness' identifies. How does one get from a motivational theory based on individual self-interest, to some broader idea of the good society? The fact (which Layard and others draw attention to) that the increase in average incomes which the market can generate does not seem to produce a corresponding increase of the general happiness arises precisely from basing the organisation of society on this conception of human nature. Bentham hoped that this contradiction could be resolved through the power of the state, through legislation. He thought that if the appropriate rewards and sanctions were set in place, individual self-interest and the general happiness could be reconciled. Some of New Labour's frenetic attempts to regulate behaviour, to encourage or constrain people to engage with the incentives of the market economy, can be understood as a renewal of this utilitarian programme, and as a way of resolving this inherent contradiction within market societies.

The shallowness of a psychological model which has been extrapolated from the discipline of economics is further revealed in Layard's discussion of the problems of mental illness and depression. He has demonstrated powerful *social* reasons why individuals might be more anxious and depressed in increasingly insecure, consumption-dominated societies. It seems logical to conclude therefore that mental illness is most likely to diminish when these *social* factors are addressed. One might think that Layard's concern about the high incidence of depression in our society would give some urgency to his arguments with the market. But in fact, he has chosen to give his main political priority to an intervention in the field of mental health: he is an advocate of the large-scale provision of cognitive behaviour therapy. In his view, CBT is the proven cure for 60 per cent of clinically depressed patients, and at a very limited cost - only £750 per patient - thus ensuring a favourable cost-benefit ratio even in economic terms.[15] If only things were so simple!

This recommendation draws also on Layard's belief in what he calls 'positive psychology', the need for and possibility of ridding the mind of negative thoughts, and replacing them with positive ones, through various methods of self-reflection - which include both CBT and Buddhist meditation. These sections of Layard's book seem rather naive, and poorly connected with his major social argument. Here is a whole society, in his view, where individuals feel so rivalrous that their own sense of well-being is impoverished by knowledge of others' good, but in which a short course of positive thinking could cure most of the clinically depressed! Although he is critical of the earlier take-over of economic thinking by the psychological assumptions of behaviourism, his

---

15. There may be an affinity between the priority given by Layard to a large-scale cognitive behaviour therapy programme, and his and New Labour's continuing commitment to 'welfare to work', since plainly depression must be significantly related to long-term unemployment or incapacity, both as its effect and as its cause (for more on governmental attitudes to incapacity benefit see Jonathan Rutherford in this issue). In the Reform of the Poor Law of 1834, the earlier utilitarians sought to enforce participation in the labour force through economic constraints and the end of unconditional assistance. Now, in this more psychological age, the will to participate needs to be addressed also, and depression undermines the will. Utilitarianism has long been aligned with what Foucauldians refer to as governmentality - with regimes of social power.

own psychological framework seems only slightly more sophisticated than this. Elsewhere, Layard, who is generally hostile to psychoanalysis, acknowledges (citing Freud) the great importance of early family experiences (as well as genetic inheritance) in forming personalities, and attaches importance to supportive relationships within families. Why would one suppose, given this, and the 'situational rationality' of anxiety and depression in the social conditions which Layard describes, that mass provision of a psychological technique designed to induce positive thinking is likely to match up to this serious problem? It would seem more to the point to address the fundamental problems of family relationships and economic security. In fact Layard's passages on 'positive thinking' remind one of nothing so much as Samuel Smiles's advocacy of self-help and its many equivalents in popular psychological literature.

The idea of giving greater priority to mental health services is of course welcome, and without doubt CBT has a useful role in such services. But the emphasis which Layard gives to these recommendations over all others seems to me the equivalent of attempting to remedy a high incidence of traffic accidents by providing more garages for the repair of cars, and more A&E Departments for the repair of their drivers and passengers, instead of addressing the reasons why so many vehicles are causing deaths and injuries in the first place. In this his approach seems similar to many other 'New Labour' policy interventions; while sometimes well-intentioned in themselves, they frequently serve to distract our attention from the 'main line' of pro-market policies that are exacerbating the deep problems which such 'micro-solutions' attempt to cure.

This article is an edited version of a talk given at a Tavistock Clinic Policy Seminar in March 2007. Comments welcome at m.j.rustin@uel.ac.uk.

Nanotechnology and visions of the future

Richard A.L. Jones

Richard Jones offers a user-friendly guide to the science that underlies nanotechnology and the debates that surround it.

Few new technologies have been accompanied by such expansive promises of their potential to change the world as nanotechnology. For some, it will lead to a utopia, in which material want has been abolished and disease is a thing of the past, while others see apocalypse and even the extinction of the human race. Governments and multinationals round the world see nanotechnology as an engine of economic growth, while campaigning groups foresee environmental degradation and a widening of the gap between the rich and poor. But at the heart of these arguments lies a striking lack of consensus about what the technology is or will be, what it will make possible and what its dangers might be. Technologies don't exist or develop in a vacuum, and nanotechnology is no exception; arguments about the likely, or indeed desirable, trajectory of the technology are as much about their protagonists' broader aspirations for society as about nanotechnology itself.

The nanoscale
Nanotechnology is not a single technology in the way that nuclear technology, agricultural biotechnology, or semiconductor technology are. There is, as yet, no

distinctive class of artefacts that can be unambiguously labelled as the product of nanotechnology. It is still, by and large, an activity carried out in laboratories rather than factories. The distinctive output of nanotechnology is the production and characterisation of some kind of device, rather than the kind of furthering of fundamental understanding that we would expect from a classical discipline such as physics or chemistry.

What unites the rather disparate group of applied sciences that are referred to as nanotechnologies is simply the length-scale on which they operate. Nanotechnology concerns the creation and manipulation of objects whose size lies somewhere between a nanometer and a few hundred nanometers. To put these numbers in context - as unaided humans we operate over a range of length-scales, which we could call the macroscale. Thus the largest objects we can manipulate unaided are about a meter or so in size, while the smallest objects we can manipulate comfortably are about one millimetre; the scale can therefore be seen as spanning a factor of a thousand or so. With the aid of light microscopes and tools for micromanipulation, we can also operate on a set of smaller length scales, which also spans a factor of a thousand. The upper end of the microscale is thus defined by a millimetre, while the lower end is defined by objects about a micron in size. This is roughly the size of a red blood cell or a typical bacteria, and is about the smallest object that can be easily discerned in a light microscope.

The nanoscale is smaller yet. A micron is one thousand nanometers, and one nanometer is about the size of a medium size molecule. So we can think of the lower limit of the nanoscale as being defined by the size of individual atoms and molecules, while the upper limit is defined by the resolution limits of light microscopes (this limit is somewhat more vague; one sometimes sees apparently more exact definitions, such as 100 nm, but these in my view are entirely arbitrary).

A number of special features make operating in the nanoscale distinctive. Firstly, there is the question of the tools one needs to see nanoscale structures and to characterise them. Conventional light microscopes cannot resolve structures this small. Electron microscopes can achieve atomic resolution, but they are expensive, difficult to use and 'prone to artefacts'.[1] However a new class

---

1. An artefact is something that appears in an image reflecting some non-ideality in the way the instrument works rather than anything real in the object that is being looked at.

of techniques that can probe the nanoscale - scanning probe microscopies, such as scanning tunnelling microscopy and atomic force microscopy - has recently become available, and the uptake of these relatively cheap and accessible methods has been a big factor in creating the field of nanotechnology.

More fundamentally, the properties of matter themselves often change in interesting and unexpected ways when their dimensions are shrunk to the nanoscale. As a particle becomes smaller, it becomes proportionally more influenced by its surface, which often leads to increases in chemical reactivity. These changes may be highly desirable - for example yielding better catalysts, for effecting chemical transformations more efficiently; or they may be undesirable, in that they can lead to increased toxicity. Quantum mechanical effects can also become important, particularly in the way electrons and light interact, and this can lead to striking and useful effects such as size dependent colour changes. (It's worth stressing here that while quantum mechanics is counter-intuitive and somewhat mysterious to the uninitiated, it is very well understood and produces definite and quantitative predictions. One sometimes reads that the laws of physics 'don't apply' at the nanoscale. This of course is quite wrong; the laws apply just as they do on any other scale, but sometimes they have different consequences.) The continuous restless activity of Brownian motion, which is the manifestation of heat energy at the nanoscale, is dominating at this scale.[2] These differences in the way physics works at the nanoscale offer opportunities to achieve new effects, but they also mean that our intuitions may not always be reliable.

One further feature of the nanoscale is that it is the length scale on which the basic machinery of biology operates. Modern molecular biology and biophysics has revealed a great deal about the sub-cellular apparatus of life, revealing the structure and mode of operation of the astonishingly sophisticated molecular-scale machines that are the basis of all organisms. This is significant in a number of ways. Cell biology provides an existence proof that it is possible to make sophisticated machines on the nanoscale, and it provides a model for making such machines. It even provides a toolkit of components that can be isolated from living cells and reassembled in synthetic contexts - this is the enterprise of bionanotechnology. The correspondence of length scales also

---

2. Brownian motion is the random movement of nano- and micro-scale particles as a result of collisions with the atoms or molecules composing the fluid they are immersed in.

brings hope that nanotechnology will make it possible to make very specific and targeted interventions into biological systems, leading, it is hoped, to new and powerful methods for medical diagnostics and therapeutics.

The history of nanotechonology: Feynman to Drexler

Nanotechnology, then, is an eclectic mix of disciplines, including elements of chemistry, physics, materials science, electrical engineering, biology and biotechnology. The way this new discipline has emerged from many existing disciplines is itself very interesting, as it illustrates an evolution of the way science is organised and practised that has occurred largely in response to external events.

The founding myth of nanotechnology places its origin in a lecture given by the American physicist Richard Feynman in 1959, published in 1960 under the title 'There's plenty of room at the bottom'. This didn't explicitly use the word nanotechnology, but it expressed in visionary and exciting terms the many technical possibilities that would open up if one was able to manipulate matter and make engineering devices on the nanoscale. This lecture is widely invoked by enthusiasts for nanotechnology of all types as laying down the fundamental challenges of the subject; and its importance is endorsed by the iconic status of Feynman as perhaps the greatest native-born American physicist. However, it seems that the identification of this lecture as a foundational document is retrospective, as there is not much evidence that it made a great deal of impact at the time. Feynman himself did not devote very much further work to these ideas, and the paper was rarely cited until the 1990s.

The word nanotechnology itself was coined by the Japanese scientist Norio Taniguchi in 1974, in the context of ultra-high precision machining. However, the writer who unquestionably propelled the word and the idea into the mainstream was K. Eric Drexler. Drexler wrote a popular and best-selling book *Engines of Creation*, published in 1986, which launched a futuristic and radical vision of a nanotechnology, one that saw it as capable of transforming all aspects of society. In Drexler's vision, which explicitly invoked Feynman's lecture, tiny *assemblers* would be able to take apart and put together any type of matter atom by atom. It would be possible to make any kind of product or artefact from its component atoms at virtually no cost, leading to the end of scarcity, and possibly the end of the money economy. Medicine would be revolutionised;

tiny robots would be able to repair the damage caused by illness or injury at the level of individual molecules and individual cells. This could lead to the effective abolition of ageing and death, while a seamless integration of physical and cognitive prostheses would lead to new kinds of enhanced humans. On the downside, free-living, self-replicating assemblers could escape into the wild, outcompete natural life-forms by virtue of their superior materials and design, and transform the earth's ecosphere into 'grey goo'. Thus, in the vision of Drexler, nanotechnology was introduced as a technology of such potential power that it could lead either to the transfiguration of humanity or to its extinction.

There are some interesting and significant themes underlying this radical, 'Drexlerite' conception of nanotechnology. One of them is the idea of matter as software. Implicit in Drexler's worldview is the idea that the nature of all matter can be reduced to a set of coordinates of its constituent atoms. Just as music can be coded in digital form on a CD or MP3 file, and moving images can be reduced to a string of bits, it's possible to imagine any object, whether an everyday tool, a priceless artwork, or even a natural product, being coded as a string of atomic coordinates. Nanotechnology, in this view, provides an interface between the software world and the physical world; an '*assembler*' or '*nanofactory*' generates an object just as a digital printer reproduces an image from its digital, software representation. It is this analogy that seems to make the Drexlerian notion of nanotechnology so attractive to the information technology community.

Predictions of what these '*nanofactories*' might look like have a very mechanistic feel to them. *Engines of Creation* had little in the way of technical detail supporting it, and included some imagery that felt quite organic and biological. However, following the popular success of *Engines*, Drexler developed his ideas at a more detailed level, publishing another, much more technical book in 1992, called *Nanosystems*. This develops a conception of nanotechnology as mechanical engineering shrunk to atomic dimensions, and it is in this form that the idea of nanotechnology has entered the popular consciousness, through science fiction, films and video games. Perhaps the best of all these cultural representations is Neal Stephenson's science fiction novel *The Diamond Age*, in which a conscious evocation of a future shaped by a return to Victorian values rather appropriately mirrors the highly mechanical feel of Drexler's conception of nanotechnology.

Is radical nanotechnology possible?

The next major development in nanotechnology was arguably political rather than visionary or scientific. In 2000 President Clinton announced a National Nanotechnology Initiative, with funding of $497 million a year. This initiative survived, and even thrived on, the change of administration in the USA, receiving further support, and funding increases, from President Bush. Following this very public initiative from the USA, other governments around the world - and the EU - have similarly announced major funding programmes. Perhaps the most interesting aspect of this international enthusiasm for nanotechnology at government level is the degree to which it is shared by countries outside those parts of North America, Europe and the Pacific Rim that are traditionally associated with a high intensity of research and development. India, China, Brazil, Iran and South Africa have all designated nanotechnology as a priority area, and in the case of China at least there is some evidence that their performance and output in nanotechnology is beginning to approach or surpass that of some Western countries, including the UK.

Some of the rhetoric associated with the US National Nanotechnology Initiative in its early days was reminiscent of the vision of Drexler. Notably, an early document was entitled *Nanotechnology: shaping the world atom by atom*. Perhaps it was useful that such a radical vision for the world-changing potential of nanotechnology was present in the background; even if it was not often explicitly invoked, neither did scientists go out of their way to refute it.

This changed in September 2001, when a special issue of the American popular science magazine *Scientific American* contained a number of contributions that were stingingly critical of the Drexler vision of nanotechnology. The most significant of these were by the Harvard nano-chemist George Whitesides, and the Rice University chemist Richard Smalley. Both argued that the Drexler vision of nanoscale machines was simply impossible on technical grounds. Smalley's contribution was perhaps the most resonant. Smalley had won a Nobel prize for the discovery of a new form of nanoscale carbon, Buckminster fullerene, and so his contribution carried significant weight.[3]

---

3. Nobel Prize for chemistry, 1996, shared with his Rice colleague Robert Curl and the British chemist Sir Harold Kroto, from Sussex University.

The dispute between Smalley and Drexler ran for a while longer, with a published exchange of letters, but its tone became increasingly vituperative. Nonetheless, the result has been that Drexler's ideas have been largely discredited in both scientific and business circles. The attitude of many scientists is summed up by IBM's Don Eigler, the first person to demonstrate the controlled manipulation of individual atoms: 'To a person, everyone I know who is a practicing scientist thinks of Drexler's contributions as wrong at best, dangerous at worse. There may be scientists who feel otherwise, I just haven't run into them.'[4]

D rexler has thus become a very polarising figure. My own view is that this is unfortunate. I believe that Drexler and his followers have greatly underestimated the technical obstacles in the way of his vision of shrunken mechanical engineering. Drexler does deserve credit, though, for pointing out that the remarkable nanoscale machinery of cell biology does provide an existence proof that a sophisticated nanotechnology is possible. However, I think he went on to draw the wrong conclusion from this. Drexler's position is essentially that we will be able greatly to surpass the capabilities of biological nanotechnology - by using rational engineering principles, rather than the vagaries of evolution, to design these machines, and by using stiff and strong materials rather than the soft and floppy proteins and membranes of biology. I believe that this fails to recognise the fact that physics does look very different at the nanoscale, and that the design principles used in biology are optimised by evolution for this different environment.[5] From this, it follows that a radical nanotechnology might well be possible, but that it will look much more like biology than engineering.

Whether or in what form radical nanotechnology does turn out to be possible, much of what is currently on the market described as nanotechnology is very much more incremental in character. Products such as nano-enabled sunscreens, anti-stain fabric coatings, or 'anti-ageing' creams certainly do not have anything to do with sophisticated nanoscale machines; instead they feature materials, coatings and structures which have some dimensions controlled on

---

4. Quoted by Chris Toumey in 'Apostolic Succession: Does Nanotechnology Descend From Richard Feynman's 1959 Talk?', *Engineering and Science*, No 1/2, 2005, p16.
5. This is essentially the argument of my own book *Soft Machines: Nanotechnology and life,* R.A.L. Jones, OUP 2004.

the nanoscale. These are useful and even potentially lucrative products, but they certainly do not represent any discontinuity with previous technology.

Between the mundane current applications of incremental nanotechnology, and the implausible speculations of the futurists, there are areas in which it is realistic to hope for substantial impacts from nanotechnology. Perhaps the biggest impacts will be seen in the three areas of energy, healthcare and information technology.

I t's clear that there will be a huge emphasis in the coming years on finding new, more sustainable ways to obtain and transmit energy. Nanotechnology could make many contributions in areas like better batteries and fuel cells, but its biggest impact could be in making solar energy economically viable on a large scale. The problem with conventional solar cells is not efficiency, but cost and manufacturing scalability. Plenty of solar energy lands on the earth, but the total area of conventional solar cells produced each year is orders of magnitude too small to make a significant dent in the world's total energy budget. New types of solar cell using nanotechnology, and drawing inspiration from the natural process of photosynthesis, are in principle compatible with large area, low cast processing techniques like printing, and it's not unrealistic to imagine this kind of solar cell being produced in huge plastic sheets at very low cost.

In medicine, if the vision of cell-by-cell surgery using nanosubmarines isn't going to happen, the prospect of the effectiveness of drugs being increased and their side-effects greatly reduced through the use of nanoscale delivery devices is much more realistic. Much more accurate and fast diagnosis of diseases is also in prospect.

One area in which nanotechnology can already be said to be present in our lives is information technology. The continuous miniaturisation of computing devices has already reached the nanoscale, and this is reflected in the growing impact of information technology on all aspects of the life of most people in the West. It's interesting that the economic driving force for the continued development of information technologies is no longer computing in its traditional sense, but largely entertainment, through digital music players, digital imaging and video. The continual shrinking of current technologies will probably continue through the dynamic of Moore's law for ten or fifteen years, allowing at least another hundred-fold increase in computing power.[6] But at this point,

---

6. Moore's law is the observation that the number of transistors (and thus, roughly, the computer power) of a silicon chip doubles every two years or so.

a number of limits, both physical and economic, are likely to provide serious impediments to further miniaturisation. New nanotechnologies may alter this picture in two ways however. It is possible, but by no means certain, that entirely new computing concepts such as quantum computing or molecular electronics may lead to new types of computer of unprecedented power, permitting the further continuation or even acceleration of Moore's law. On the other hand, developments in plastic electronics may make it possible to make computers that are not especially powerful, but which are very cheap or even disposable. It is this kind of development that is likely to facilitate the idea of 'ubiquitous computing' or 'the internet of things', in which it is envisaged that every artefact and product incorporates a computer able to sense its surroundings and to communicate wirelessly with its neighbours. One can see that as a natural, even inevitable, development of technologies like the radio frequency identification devices (RFID) already used as 'smart barcodes' by shops like Walmart, but it is clear also that some of the scenarios envisaged could lead to serious concerns about loss of privacy and, potentially, civil liberties.

Transhumanism

There are many debates about nanotechnology - what it is, what it will make possible, and what its dangers might be. On one level these may seem to be very technical in nature. So a question about whether a Drexler style assembler is technically feasible can rapidly descend into details of surface chemistry, while issues about the possible toxicity of carbon nanotubes turn on the procedures for reliable toxicological screening. But it's at least arguable that the focus on the technical obscures the real causes of the argument, which are actually based on clashes of ideology. What are the ideological divisions that underlie debates about nanotechnology?

Underlying the most radical visions of nanotechnology is an equally radical ideology - transhumanism. The basis of this movement is a teleological view of human progress which views technology as the vehicle, not just for the improvement of the lot of humanity, but for the transcendence of the kind of limitation that non-transhumanists would consider to be an inevitable part of the human condition. The most pressing of these limitations, of course, is death, so transhumanists look forward to nanotechnology providing a permanent solution to this problem. In the first instance, this will be effected by nanomedicine, which they anticipate as making cell-by-cell repairs to any damage possible. Beyond this, some transhumanists believe that computers of such power will become available that they will constitute true artificial intelligence. At this point, they imagine a merging of human and machine intelligence, in a way that would effectively constitute the evolution of a new and improved version of humankind.

'radical futurism has put nanotechnology into popular culture but it is the prospect of money that has excited business and government'

The notion that the pace of technological change is continually accelerating is an article of faith amongst transhumanists. This leads to the idea that this accelerating rate of change will lead to a point beyond which the future is literally inconceivable. This point they refer to as 'the singularity', and discussions of this hypothetical event take on a highly eschatological tone. This is captured in science fiction writer Cory Doctorow's dismissive but apt phrase for the singularity: 'the rapture of the nerds'.

This worldview carries with it the implication that an accelerating pace of innovation is not just a historical fact, but also a moral imperative. This is because it is through technology that humanity will achieve its destiny, which is nothing less that to transcend its own current physical and mental limitations. The achievement of radical nanotechnology is central to this project, and for this reason transhumanists tend to share a strong conviction not only that radical nanotechnology along Drexlerian lines is possible, but also that its development is morally necessary.

Transhumanism can be considered to be the extreme limit of views that combine strong technological determinism with a highly progressive view of the development of humanity. It is a worldwide movement, but it's probably fair to say that its natural home is California, its main constituency is amongst those involved in information technology, and it is associated predominantly, if not exclusively, with a strongly libertarian streak of politics - though, paradoxically, not dissimilar views seem to be attractive to a certain class of former Marxists.

Given that transhumanism as an ideology does not seem to have a great deal of mass appeal, it's tempting to underplay its importance. This may be a mistake. Amongst its adherents are a number of figures with very high media profiles, particularly in the United States, and transhumanist ideas have entered mass culture through science fiction, films and video games. Certainly some conservative and religious figures have felt threatened enough to express some alarm, notably Francis Fukuyama, who has described transhumanism as 'the world's most dangerous idea'.

Global capitalism and the changing innovation landscape

If it is the radical futurism of the transhumanists that has put nanotechnology into popular culture, it is the prospect of money that has excited business and government. Nanotechnology is seen by many worldwide as the major driver of economic growth over the next twenty years, filling the role that information technology has filled over the last twenty years. Breathless projections of huge new markets are commonplace, with the prediction by the US National Nanotechnology Initiative of a trillion dollar market for nanotechnology products by 2015 being the most notorious of these. It is this kind of market projection that underlies a worldwide spending boom on nanotechnology research, which encompasses both the established science and technology powerhouses such as the USA, Germany and Japan, and fast developing countries like China and India.

The emergence of nanotechnology has corresponded with some other interesting changes in the commercial landscape in technologically intensive sectors of the economy. The types of incremental nanotechnology that have been successfully commercialised so far have involved nanoparticles, such as the ones used in sunscreens, or coatings, of the kind used in stain-resistant fabrics. This sort of innovation is the province of the speciality chemicals sector, and one cynical view of the prominence of the nanotechnology label amongst new and old companies is that it has allowed companies in this rather unfashionable sector of the market to rebrand themselves as part of the newest new thing, with correspondingly higher stock market valuations and easier access to capital. On the other hand, this does perhaps signal a more general change in the way science-driven innovations reach the market.

Many of the large industrial conglomerates that were so prominent in the industrial landscape of Western countries up to the 1980s have been broken up or drastically shrunken. Arguably, the monopoly rents that sustained these combines were what made possible the very large and productive corporate laboratories that were the source of much innovation at that time. This has been replaced by a much more fluid scene, in which many functions of companies, including research and innovation, have been outsourced. In this landscape, one finds nanotechnology companies - such as Oxonica - which are essentially holding companies for intellectual property; such companies frequently outsource to contractors, often located in different countries, functions that in the past would have been regarded as of core importance, such as manufacturing and marketing.

Even the remaining large companies have embraced the concept of 'open innovation', in which research and development is regarded as a commodity to be purchased on the open market (and, indeed, outsourced to low cost countries), rather than as a core function of the corporation. It is in this light that one should understand the new prominence of intellectual property as something fungible and readily monetised. Universities and other public research institutes, strongly encouraged to seek new sources of funding other than direct government support, have made increasing efforts to spin-out new companies based on intellectual property developed by academic researchers.

In the light of all this, it's easy to see nanotechnology as one aspect of a more general shift to what the social scientist Michael Gibbons has called Mode II knowledge production.[7] In this view, traditional academic values are being eclipsed by a move to more explicitly goal-oriented and highly interdisciplinary research, in which research priorities are set not by the values of the traditional disciplines, but by perceived market needs and opportunities. It is clear that this transition has been underway for some time in the life sciences, and in this view the emergence of nanotechnology can be seen as a spread of these values to the physical sciences.

Opposition

In the UK at least, the opposition to nanotechnology has been spearheaded by two unlikely bedfellows. The issue was first propelled into the news by the intervention of Prince Charles, who raised the subject in newspaper articles in 2003 and 2004. These articles directly echoed concerns raised by the small campaigning group ETC,[8] who cast nanotechnology as a direct successor to genetic modification. To summarise this framing, the argument is that, whereas in GM scientists had

---

7. M. Gibbons et al, *The New Production of Knowledge*, Sage 1994.
8. David Berube (in his book *Nano-hype*, Prometheus, NY 2006) explicitly links the two interventions, and identifies Zac Goldsmith, millionaire organic farmer and editor of *The Ecologist* magazine, as the man who introduced Prince Charles to nanotechnology and the ETC critique. This could be significant, in view of Goldsmith's current prominence in Conservative Party politics.

directly intervened in the code of life, in nanotechnology they meddle with the very atomic structure of matter itself. ETC's background included a strong record of campaigning on behalf of third world farmers against agricultural biotechnology, and in their view nanotechnology - with its spectre of the possible patenting of new arrangements of atoms and the potential replacement of commodities such as copper and cotton by nanoengineered substitutes controlled by multinationals - was to be opposed as an intrinsic part of the agenda of globalisation. Complementing this rather abstract critique was a much more concrete concern that nanoscale materials might be more toxic than their conventional counterparts, and that current regulatory regimes for the control of environmental exposure to chemicals might not adequately recognise these new dangers.

The latter concern has gained a considerable degree of traction, largely because there has been a very widespread degree of consensus that the issue has some substance. At the time of the Prince's intervention in the debate (and quite possibly because of it), the UK government commissioned a high-level independent report on the issue from the Royal Society and the Royal Academy of Engineering. This report recommended a programme of research and regulatory action on the subject of possible nanoparticle toxicity.[9] Public debate about the risks of nanotechnology has largely focused on this issue, fuelled by a government response to the Royal Society that has been widely considered to be quite inadequate. However, it is possible to regret that the debate has become so focused on this rather technical issue of risk, to the exclusion of wider issues about the potential impacts of nanotechnology on society.

To return to the more fundamental worldviews underlying this critique of nanotechnology, whether they be the rather romantic, ruralist conservatism of the Prince of Wales, or the anti-globalism of ETC, the common feature is a general scepticism about the benefits of scientific and technological 'progress'. An extremely eloquent exposition of one version of this point of view is to be found in a book by US journalist Bill McKibben, *Enough*, whose title is a succinct summary of its argument.[10] McKibben argues that we now have enough technology for our needs, and that new technology is likely only to lead to further

---

9. *Nanoscience and nanotechnologies: opportunities and uncertainties*, Royal Society and Royal Academy of Engineering, available from www.nanotec.org.uk/finalReport.htm.

10. *Enough; staying human in an engineered age*, Bill McKibben, Henry Hall 2003.

spiritual malaise, through excessive consumerism, or in the case of new and very powerful technologies like genetic modification and nanotechnology, to new and terrifying existential dangers.

Despite the worries about the toxicology of nanoscale particles, and the involvement of groups like ETC, it is notable that all-out opposition to nanotechnology has not yet fully crystallised. In particular, groups such as Greenpeace have not yet articulated a position of unequivocal opposition. This reflects the fact that nanotechnology really does seem to have the potential to provide answers to some pressing environmental problems. For example, there are real hopes that it will lead to new types of solar cells that can be produced cheaply in very large areas. Applications of nanotechnology to problems of water purification and desalination have obvious potential impacts in parts of the world where water supply infrastructure is weak. Of course, these kinds of applications have major political and social dimensions, and technical fixes by themselves will not be sufficient. However, the prospects that nanotechnology may be able to make a significant contribution to sustainable development have proved convincing enough to keep mainstream environmental movements at least neutral on the issue.

While some mainstream environmentalists remain equivocal in their view of nanotechnology, another group seems to be embracing new technologies with some enthusiasm, as providing new ways of maintaining high standards of living in a fully sustainable way. Such 'bright greens' dismiss the rejection of industrialised economies and yearning to return to a rural lifestyle that is implicit in the 'deep green' worldview, and look to the use of new technology, together with imaginative design and planning, to create sustainable urban societies.[11] In this point of view, nanotechnology may help, not just by enabling large scale solar power, but by facilitating an intrinsically less wasteful industrial ecology.

Conclusion

If such a thing exists (or indeed ever existed) as an 'independent republic of science', disinterestedly pursuing knowledge for its own sake, nanotechnology

---

11. For a recent manifesto, see *Worldchanging: a user's guide for the 21st century*, Alex Steffen (ed.), Harry N. Abrams 2006.

is not part of it. Nanotechnology, in all its flavours and varieties, is unashamedly 'goal-oriented research'. This immediately begs the question 'whose goals?' It is this question that underlies recent calls for a greater degree of democratic involvement in setting scientific priorities.[12] It is important that these debates don't simply concentrate on technical issues. Nanotechnology provides a fascinating and evolving example of the complexity of the interaction between science, technology and wider currents in society. Nanotechnology, with other new and emerging technologies, will have a huge impact on the way society develops over the next twenty to fifty years. Recognising the importance of this impact, however, does not by any means imply that one must take a technologically deterministic view of the future. Technology co-evolves with society, and the direction it takes is not necessarily pre-determined. Underlying the directions in which it is steered is a set of competing visions about the directions society should take. These ideologies, which often are left implicit and unexamined, need to be made explicit if a meaningful discussion of the implications of the technology is to take place.

---

12. See for example *See-through Science: why public engagement needs to move upstream*, Rebecca Willis and James Wilsdon, Demos 2004.

The politics of time

Valerie Bryson

Valerie Bryson argues for resistance to the results-oriented 'clock-time' of the capitalist economy.

In recent years, a number of time related issues have risen up the political agenda in the UK. Concern about the damaging effects of long working hours is widely articulated. The TUC's 'It's About Time' campaign aims to put long hours and work/life balance at the top of the workplace agenda,[1] many feminists see such workplace reform as a precondition for sex equality, and politicians across the political spectrum claim to support flexible, 'family-friendly' working conditions. And, partly because of EU pressure, there has been a series of measures since 1997 providing workers with more family leave entitlements, some legal protection against excessively long hours, and more opportunity to work flexible hours.

This article discusses the alleged ill effects of long working hours, before digging below the surface debates to look at time itself in more detail. It argues that we experience and relate to time in many ways, but that our society is dominated by one particular kind of time - the measurable, results-oriented clock time of the capitalist economy. Failure to recognise other temporal needs and rhythms, particularly those associated with caring responsibilities, has damaging social effects, and it also reflects - and sustains - deep-seated gender inequalities. Tackling the dominant time culture and asserting the value of other kinds of time is a critical political step that casts fresh light on current inequalities and opens up new ways of thinking about a more humane and equitable society.

---

1. See the 'Changing Times' website on www.tuc.org.uk/work_life/index.cfm?mins=377.

So little time, so much to do …

Contrary to the widespread expectation that technology would liberate us from toil, we now seem to be working harder than ever before. Surveys repeatedly find that people feel overworked and too busy, with not enough time for their families, their friends or themselves, and new terms such as 'time poverty', 'time famine' and 'hurry sickness' have been coined to describe their sense of stress. In this context, it is at first sight surprising to find that there has been a long-term *decline* in average working hours. However, this trend has been countered by a steady increase in time spent travelling to work and by an increase in women's employment, so that in many households less adult time is available to run the home and care for family members; rising life expectancy also means that an increasing number of workers have caring responsibilities for elderly parents. State support for family responsibilities falls far short of what is needed, and this produces a significant 'care deficit' and a 'time squeeze' in many households, as people struggle to juggle the needs of workplace and family.

A significant minority of employees continue to work extremely long hours, with around 4 million working over 48 hours in an average week, and around 1 in 6 working 60 hours. While some long-hours workers welcome the opportunity to earn overtime, a majority say they would prefer to work shorter hours but are unaware that they have a legal right to do so. Some fear that, in a culture of 'presenteeism' and job insecurity, their career will suffer or they will lose their job if they refuse overtime. Many work unpaid overtime because they are simply required to do more work than can be fitted into a 40 hour week; and many have become trapped in a work-to-spend cycle in an economy that treats growth as an end in itself and sees any decline in consumption as a sign of recession.

According to many commentators, the resulting time pressures are having damaging effects on individuals, their families and society as a whole, contributing to a range of physical and mental health problems, a breakdown in social cohesion and a decline in economic effectiveness and civic engagement. Meanwhile, government ministers and public officials exhort us to take more interest in politics, eat fresh vegetables rather than convenience foods, read more with our children, walk them to school, keep an eye on our elderly neighbours, act as school governors, take more exercise, get more involved in our local communities - while not forgetting that our primary role as citizens is to participate as members of the paid workforce and avoid depending on state benefits. The hours simply do not add up - people cannot work the hours that full-time employment so often demands if they have family responsibilities and are active members of their community.

Political theorists and commentators have long recognised that money is an unequally distributed political resource whose possession provides access to power and influence. They have, however, generally failed to see that free time is also a political resource, and that this too is both scarce and unequally distributed. If citizens are constantly pressed for time, civic life will suffer, and groups whose time poverty is most acute will find it particularly hard to get a political voice. As discussed in the next sections, some feminists have identified time pressures as a key factor behind women's continuing economic disadvantage and political under-representation.

Inequality begins at home

The discussion so far has, as is conventional, equated 'work' with paid employment. However, many unpaid domestic activities also constitute work in the sense that they could in principle be done by a paid worker; many are also essential to the survival and well-being of society. They are also time-consuming, and if someone is cleaning, cooking or looking after children they cannot at the same time be working for money, attending a political meeting or enjoying free time. Some feminists have successfully argued that this invisible work should be recognised in government economic statistics, and at the end of the 1995 UN World Conference on Women in Beijing, many governments (including the UK) agreed to conduct regular time-use studies as a way of measuring and valuing unpaid work.

Such studies confirm both that unpaid work is economically valuable and that, although men in western societies do significantly more in the home than they used to, this does not match the increase in women's paid employment hours and falls far short of domestic equality. Many feminists claim that women's 'double shift' of paid and unpaid work leaves them little time for political involvement: contrary to earlier feminist hopes, women seem not to be 'having it all' but 'doing it all'. Indeed, it seems that little has really changed since the British suffrage campaigner and socialist Hannah Mitchell famously complained, nearly one hundred years ago, that: 'No cause can be won between dinner and tea, and most of us who were married had to fight with one hand tied behind us'.[2]

Given their ascribed family responsibilities and current conditions of employment, many UK women opt out of pursuing a career, choosing instead the 'Mummy track' of less demanding and/or part-time work, or dropping out of the labour market, when their children are young. This pattern has negative consequences for the economy, as women's abilities are under-utilised. It also means that many women are at least partially economically dependent on a male partner's wage, and that over a quarter of women in the UK have no independent income at all; women are also more likely than men to live in poverty. Such dependency and poverty are incompatible with the status of full citizenship and are linked to women's continuing political under-representation. They reflect a failure to recognise the value of women's contribution to society, or to see that many apparently independent male citizens are in fact care receivers, dependent on the time of those who service their daily needs. One consequence is that an increasing number of highly educated young women appear to be choosing not to have children, rather than losing their independence and/or struggling to combine work and family life.

Many feminists have long campaigned for changes in conditions of employment, so that women can more readily combine reasonably paid employment with domestic responsibilities; they are also increasingly calling for men too to be enabled to contribute more in the home. Although in the UK equal opportunities has usually been seen as allowing women to compete with men on existing terms, these arguments are at last feeding into policies. Not only has maternity leave been extended significantly in recent years; fathers too now have a right to some paternity leave, new entitlements to parental leave are in principle open to men, workers with family responsibilities are entitled to have requests for flexible working considered, and conditions of part-time employment have improved.

Welcome though these measures are, they do not challenge the 'normality' of the long hours that a successful career so often demands, and that can only readily be worked by those whose domestic needs and responsibilities are met by someone else. Given the traditional allocation of time and responsibilities, there is

---

2. H. Mitchell, *The Hard Way Up*, Virago 1997, p130.

a danger that they will be seen as policies for women only, leaving men's 'domestic absenteeism' and workplace advantages unquestioned, particularly as new fathers are eligible for very limited leave compared to mothers. Scandinavian experience suggests that generous maternity leave actually strengthens traditionally gendered responsibilities; it is only when a period of parental leave is reserved for men (as currently in Norway, Sweden and Iceland) that men become significantly more involved. The 'gender equality duty' that came into force in the UK in April 2007, and requires all public bodies to demonstrate that they are actively promoting equality for women and men, is likely to lead to some improvements.

However, long hours and a culture of 'presenteeism' remain endemic in the private sector; maternity and parental leave provision still lags behind most of Europe; and UK workers retain the right to opt-out of the 48 hour maximum week established by the EU Working Time Directive.

Nevertheless, as a series of recent reports for the Equal Opportunities Commission makes clear, there has been a shift in men's aspirations and practices: nearly a third of fathers work flexitime in order to balance their work and family commitments, 80 per cent take leave when their child is born, and many say they would take more if they could afford to.[3] Here public opinion seems significantly ahead of the law, with a majority of citizens saying that better support for working carers, particularly fathers, is a priority, and that party policies on this would influence their vote.

What free time?

If people are to be politically active, they need 'free time', that is, time left after deducting paid and unpaid work, personal care and sleep. While the patterns are not clear-cut, access to this scarce resource often seems to reflect and sustain wider socio-economic inequalities. In particular, although time-use studies at first sight refute the feminist claim that women have significantly less free time than men, closer examination shows that women's free time is often highly fragmented and unpredictable (15 minutes in the morning if the baby doesn't wake, half an hour in the afternoon if the children play next door …). Their leisure time is also often combined with childcare, and although many mothers may appear to be free in the evening, they are likely to be 'on call' and unable

---

3. See www.eoc.org.uk/research.

to leave the house unless another adult can be there. In contrast, men's time is generally more 'usable': even if they work long hours, they are more likely to be able to arrange to meet someone after work, attend a governors' meeting or go to a weekend conference.

Similarly, although long hours working is concentrated amongst managerial and professional employees, less well paid workers lack the capacity to 'buy time' (for example by taking a taxi instead of a bus, or paying for domestic help); their working hours tend to be more inflexible, they more often have to work anti-social hours and they are less likely to be able to afford to take their family leave entitlements. These problems are compounded for working-class women, who often fit more than one poorly paid part-time job around their family responsibilities, while the redistribution of domestic and caring work from better paid families to paid workers (usually women, usually poorly paid, often migrant) shifts the 'care deficit' from economically privileged to disadvantaged families, 'freeing up' time for the former at the expense of the latter.

Time in capitalist societies

While careful use of time-use studies can help reveal patterned inequalities, time-use studies depend on a particular and limited perception of both free time and time itself. The very notion of 'free' time gained its meaning in relation to capitalist employment, in which workers generally sell their time rather than the products of their labour. It rests on the assumption that work is an alien, imposed activity, involving a loss of humanity, free expression and self-direction. As in the current rhetoric of 'work-life balance', work is seen as a sacrifice of life, undertaken only in order to earn a wage; this dominant perspective also often assumes that time left over from this is free time, available for workers to spend as they please.

Many people, particularly women, do not experience a distinction between working and free time. The sense that their time is not their own is particularly acute for those carers who are permanently 'on call', even when apparently at leisure or asleep, and for those whose 'second shift' of caring for their family occupies all their time out of paid employment. As described above, there has been a move towards re-defining such responsibilities as a form of work. However, the time they take is often forgotten, for example by those who insist that lone mothers should be in paid employment rather than dependent on state benefits. There is also a widespread sense that family responsibilities should be motivated by love alone and that they therefore should not be seen as work. Although time-use studies help reveal the time people spend on unpaid responsibilities, they do so in terms of the language of the capitalist economy; as such, they can only measure their value narrowly as exchange value or price, rather than as human worth or importance.

This point is linked to broader issues around the ways in which we experience and understand time - which seem to be culturally variable, rather than either innate, or a straightforward reflection of the natural world. Some historians have identified a significant change in human relationships with time in western societies between the fifteenth and nineteenth centuries, coinciding with the advent of capitalism and factory production. This has often been described as a shift from a traditional to a modern time culture: that is, from a natural, seasonal, local, task-oriented time, in which people got up when it was light, went to bed when it was dark, did their work according to the demands of the season and then rested, in a timeless, endless cycle, to the time of wage labourers, paid according to how long they worked rather than what they produced, with their hours and pace standardised according to the needs of the mechanical production process and the maximisation of profit. From this perspective, the commodification of labour required by capitalist production was bound up with a new form of time discipline, based on the commodification of time. This in turn depended on a view of time as an abstract, quantifiable, divisible resource that could be bought, sold, saved, invested, spent or wasted, and on the prior development of accurate mechanical clocks.

Men's time and women's time

Workers' initial resistance to the principle of time discipline soon gave way to a more limited struggle over working hours. However, although today's dominant time culture equates time with the results-oriented, commodified time of the clock, this does not exhaust our human relationship with time. Our bodies have their own temporal needs and rhythms, we experience time subjectively (it often appears to speed up or slow down), and at any moment we are never simply in the present but also in the past and future, in a mesh of hopes, fears, memories, plans and predictions.[4] More particularly, providing emotional support, or looking after

---

4. See the influential work of Barbara Adam, particularly *Timewatch*, Polity Press 1995.

children or sick or elderly adults, often requires attention to 'natural' temporal rhythms that cannot appropriately be automated or subjected to considerations of 'time management', but are often necessarily slow and in the present; the processes of feeding, cleaning, dressing and reassurance are repeated over and over again, and their timing is determined at least partly by need rather than the clock (you change the nappy because it is dirty, not because it is four o'clock).

While gender roles are fluid and variable, and we all necessarily inhabit more than one 'time culture', the traditional association of caring responsibilities with women and paid employment with men makes it meaningful to **'dropping a child off at nursery is not the same as dropping the car off at a garage'** describe these as 'women's time' and 'men's time' respectively. This description helps us link the contrast between relational/caring time and the clock time of the paid workplace with the more general privileging of men's experiences and needs. Thus, as gendered inequalities in time-use interact with differences in 'time culture', women's temporal perspectives are marginalised or ignored in public debate, and the rhythms of family life are increasingly forced to conform to the economic rationality of clock time - for example, children are rushed through dressing and breakfast so that they can get to their childminder or school on time, and parental 'to do' lists include spending set periods of 'quality time' with their family. The experience of paid care workers, expected to allocate their time strictly according to the clock and to 'switch off' when their shift is over, highlights the general difficulty of fitting the more 'natural' temporal rhythms of care into a rigid time-frame, as the intangible processes and relationships that good care involves are lost in a plethora of efficiency targets and a mountain of paperwork.

I f we assert the value of 'women's time', we can see that the physical and emotional needs of children and adults do not necessarily conform to the demands of the clock: dropping a child off at nursery is not the same as dropping the car off at a garage, relationships with partners and friends have their own, frequently unpredictable, rhythms, paid care workers cannot check properly on the welfare of a confused elderly person in a fifteen minute visit, and patients are likely to recover more quickly if the nurse who changes their sheets 'wastes' a few minutes chatting to them. The problem is not simply that people are pressed for time, and therefore find it difficult to care for others as they often wish (although this is very important); it is also that their activities are being forced into an inappropriate temporal straitjacket based on the logic of market capitalism - that is, an economic system based on the pursuit of profit rather than the satisfaction of human need or the expression of creativity.

Time-use studies and 'women's time'

While time-use studies can expose some time-related pressures, they are in danger of confirming the capitalist logic of men's time. In particular, studies based on time diaries, which are generally regarded as the most accurate, assume that we can record our days as a sequential list of discrete activities that can be assigned a monetary value. This perspective can only see care as an 'activity', with episodes of care following or succeeding episodes of paid employment or leisure. However, caring often involves simply 'being there' rather than doing something that can be recorded in a diary, while caring responsibilities can permeate the whole of a carer's life, constraining how they spend their time even when they are not actively providing care. The studies also see time as something that can be straightforwardly owned and used by individuals, ignoring its relational nature, and the extent to which usable time for some is created by the domestic work of others - including the work of planning and coordinating household timetables, most often done by women, that enables family members to participate in school, work and social life outside the home.

Even within their own terms, time-use studies have often under-estimated the 'time costs' of childcare and other caring responsibilities. Because time diaries often ask respondents to record only one activity in each time slot, they lose sight of the care that is combined with it - as when watching television or cooking a meal in the company of children.

Many recent studies, however, including the largest (2000-2001) UK national survey, have asked respondents to identify what else they were doing and whether any children or other adults were present. The resulting data shows that although parents are spending more time with their children than they used to, they partly achieve this by combining childcare with other activities, including leisure. This is particularly the case for mothers. Such 'multitasking' can be seen as a form of work intensification that would be seen as a form of increased productivity if it were paid. Its prevalence helps explain why people perceive themselves to be increasingly time pressed, even though average time in employment has declined.

Towards a politics of time

This article has been underpinned by three linked beliefs: that the ways in which time is used, valued and understood in contemporary capitalist societies are damaging the health and welfare of citizens and their families; that they make it difficult to engage in community and political activities; and that they help maintain gender inequalities in public and private life. In the interests of society as a whole, they should be challenged and changed.

The progressive 'politics of time' would have a dual starting-point. Firstly, it would expect 'normal' employees, men as well as women, to have family responsibilities and a life outside the workplace. Employment policies and pension entitlements should therefore assume that most employees will need to take leave or work reduced hours at some points in their life, and that if someone works for money for sixty hours a week they are likely to be an irresponsible citizen, neglecting their social and civic duties, and free-riding on the domestic labour of others. Secondly, it would link current debates around parental leave and flexible employment to a radical challenge to the all-encompassing nature of commodified clock time. Rejecting the assumption that all human activities can or should be organised or measured by the mechanical time of the clock, it would assert the value of time that is not measured by money, but that responds to human needs, whether these be to perform particular tasks in however long this takes, or to care for and communicate with others, or to build relationships. As part of this, it would insist that paid care workers should be treated as professionals, with a workload that recognises that good quality care cannot be delivered quickly, but involves the time-consuming development of human relationships. This means that the provision of care will not be profitable, but will have to be provided or subsidised as a public service.

Unions are likely to play a key role in pushing for these changes and to work to extend them internationally, in the knowledge that poor terms of employment elsewhere are likely to create a downwards pressure on pay and conditions. Conversely, they are likely to be opposed by powerful economic interests, not only because they may threaten short-term profitability, but also because they represent a threat to the underlying temporal logic of capitalism and the market economy. Nevertheless, the social and economic costs of workplace stress, population decline, the loss or under-utilisation of trained women workers and the growing 'care deficit' mean that employers may also have a long-term collective interest in providing more 'family-friendly' conditions of employment (although state regulation rather than simple exhortation will be needed to prevent 'good' employers being undercut by less scrupulous or far-sighted competitors). While a more radical shift to recognise and accommodate the temporal needs of human relationships may seem impossibly utopian (indeed uchronian), the cost of ignoring them may be even greater.

A de-militarised war

Faisal Devji

Faisal Devji argues that because 'terror' is an abstract concept, the war against it cannot be conducted according to military norms. This can be clearly seen in the history of Abu Ghraib.

Following the attacks of 11 September 2001 on New York and Washington, the United States and its allies used military force to topple the governments of two Muslim countries and occupy their territory. These events in Afghanistan and Iraq were complemented by the creation of a global security regime which sought to track, capture and eliminate all terrorist threats to the US and its clients, whether financial, material or human. Despite the massive amount of force deployed in its service, however, this quickly baptised War on Terror was not in fact a military operation. Even the phrase 'war on terror', after all, had a civilian rather than military genealogy in American history, deriving as it did from the metaphorical use of military action in slogans like the 'war on drugs' of the 1980s.

Like the war on drugs, crime or poverty before it, that on terror defines its enemy neither as a set of people nor as a set of ideas, but instead as the inanimate product of such agents. A traditional enemy, with or against whom one could wage war, has been replaced by a substance, or an abstraction, on which only a metaphorical war can be conducted. Indeed enemies of the old fashioned kind are notable by their absence from the War on Terror; it moved quickly from Al-Qaeda to the Taliban to Saddam Hussein and beyond, as if to demonstrate the constantly shifting shape of enmity in this new kind of conflict. It dispenses even with the ideological movement as its antagonist. For, unlike communism during the Cold War, it is terror and not terrorism that is the most frequently named target of our times, a moving target under which any sort of enemy might fall.

Given the absence of an enemy in the War on Terror, it is not surprising that the United States should conduct it by ignoring all the traditional laws of war, from issuing formal declarations to refraining from torture and assassination. But it could hardly do otherwise, since America's military might is so disproportionate in extent as to render the US incapable of waging a traditional war anyway, which is to say one fought against a foe who presents it any kind of military challenge. As the philosopher Alain Badiou puts it, the United States can no longer wage war; it can only mount enormously costly and destructive spectacles of deterrence or revenge - whether or not these secure it any geo-political advantage. In other words the War on Terror is more a police than a military operation (though we shall see that its form of policing departs from the norms of criminology, to become a conflict that occurs outside the inherited institutions of our political life).

If deterrence is generally a feature of criminal rather than military law, revenge is an aspect of criminality that exists outside the law itself. After all, one of the classical functions of a legal order is to bring private revenge to an end by substituting public justice for it. In turning to vengeance as a rhetorical and would-be political device, America does not simply violate the rule of law in its unilateral actions regarding torture or indefinite detention: it also returns to the sphere of private life governed by ethical rather than juridical precepts. This doesn't happen automatically, by reason of US power alone, but requires the participation of a particular kind of foe - one who is neither an enemy in the military sense nor a criminal in the civilian one, but instead someone who evades the terms and categories of traditional politics altogether.

I will argue here that the emergence of Al-Qaeda as a new kind of enemy has resulted in the paradoxical de-militarisation of the war waged against it - a war that can no longer be accommodated within the traditional structure of our politics. I will make this argument by discussing the much publicised incidents of abuse at the US detention centre of Abu Ghraib in 2004, to show how they provide an example of the way in which the War on Terror has increasingly become a quasi-criminal rather than a military operation. My larger point will be to suggest that this war is more and more conducted according to the civilian, as well as the strictly ethical practices of private life, which disrupt military hierarchies by their networked form.

Criminalising the enemy

The transformation of war into a species of policing, and therefore its de-militarisation, is something that has been widely recognised, not least within the US armed forces themselves. In 2004, for instance, the 'Final report of the independent panel to review Department of Defense detention operations' dealt with the incidents of prisoner abuse at Abu Ghraib precisely by placing them in this context. It argued that the emergence of global terrorism and its 'asymmetric warfare' made the 'orthodox lexicon of war' - terms such as state sovereignty, national borders, uniformed combatants, declarations of war and even war itself - irrelevant; for today, 'the power to wage war can rest in the hands of a few dozen highly motivated people with cell phones and access to the Internet.'[1]

Furthermore:

the smallness and wide dispersal of these enemy assets make it problematic to focus on signal and imagery intelligence as we did in the Cold War, Desert Storm and the first phase of Operation Iraqi Freedom. The ability of terrorists and insurgents to blend into the civilian population further decreases their vulnerability to signal and imagery intelligence. Thus, information gained from human sources, whether by spying or interrogation, is essential in narrowing the field upon which other intelligence gathering resources may be applied (Strasser, p27).

What all this means is that a place like Abu Ghraib was suddenly transformed into something it was never meant to be, an interrogation centre that was part of a new form of warfare, in which 'the distinction between front and rear becomes more fluid' (Strasser, p28). Which is to say the novelty of the global war on terror was represented at the prison by the virtual collapse of distinctions between internal and external enemies, as well as between front and rear lines.

Quite apart from the ineptitude exhibited by all concerned with the prison,

---

1. See Steven Strasser (ed), *The Abu Ghraib Investigations*, Public Affairs, 2004, p27. This book includes extracts from Pentagon and other official reports into the abuse, and is referred to hereafter in the text as Strasser.

as well as the infractions committed by some among its staff, the abuse at Abu Ghraib was important because it threw light upon the new role assumed by military detention, which was no longer to process front-line suspects quickly for distribution to judicial bodies in the rear, but rather to hold them for extended periods in order to extract urgent or 'actionable' information that might prevent future acts of terror, a function which is effectively one of policing, because it turns enemy actions into criminal ones.

Extracting information from prisoners of war is no new thing, but to do so in the theatre of war by intertwining and even confusing the jurisdiction of the army and the CIA is a departure from standard practice. The very presence of the CIA at the prison signalled the introduction there of rules outside traditional military logic as well as jurisdiction. So the facility of Abu Ghraib lost its traditional function of providing one service in the linear logic of military deployment - something like an old-fashioned factory line - to become a multi-tasking node within a non-linear or network logic.

Now it was this very criminalisation of enemy actions that had led to the partial suspension of the Geneva Conventions - including Presidential approval, in principle, of the use of torture for Al-Qaeda and Taliban detainees in Afghanistan and Guantanamo Bay. In other words, because such detainees did not seem to fall under the formal, public and state-centred categories listed by the Geneva Conventions, they could be described as unlawful combatants, enemy combatants or unprivileged belligerents.

The debate generated by these developments has focused on the fact that such new enemies appear to possess no legal status at all, being defined neither as soldiers nor as civilians, neither as foreign subjects nor as domestic ones. This was exactly the concern expressed by the International Committee of the Red Cross as well as by the US Supreme Court, since the government did not even have a negative definition for such combatants, i.e. those who could not fall into their ranks (Strasser, pp88-9).

What the debate did not take into consideration, however, is the fact that suspending any kind of juridical definition for the enemy ended up pushing him from the public status of foreigner and soldier to the private one of domestic and civilian ambiguity. In other words, because this enemy had no legal status under international or domestic statute, he existed underneath the law rather than under it. And since even a criminal enjoys rights because he possesses juridical status, this new enemy was not classed as a criminal, but only as someone like a criminal.

What this did was transform the landscape of war into one of civilian and therefore of ethical life, because the enemy was now increasingly given his due not by right but as a gift or favour. Treated thus he became a human being rather than a prisoner of war properly defined, which meant that his captors, too, were suddenly and not without irony defined merely as human beings, and not as soldiers subject to a set of positive regulations.

The precedent for such a status in American history is that of slaves, who also existed underneath the law governing free men as much as criminals, becoming therefore merely human beings along with their masters.[2] For what could be more human than social relations governed by ethical practices rather than by juridical ones based on the idea of contract? In the American context slavery as an ethical relationship arising from the absence of contractual obligations has taken on a paradigmatic name, that of Uncle Tom. Even at its source, Harriet Beecher Stowe's abolitionist novel *Uncle Tom's Cabin*, the relationship of Uncle Tom and his master is portrayed as an ethical one. Indeed it is the slave's demonstration of this ethics that allows Stowe to call for his emancipation.

Civilian ethics and the military

All this is made very clear by the presidential memorandum of 7 February 2002, which suspends certain articles of the Geneva Conventions while at the same time emphasising the need to adhere to their principles. 'As a matter of policy', the President declared, 'United States Armed Forces shall continue to treat detainees humanely and, to the extent appropriate and consistent with military necessity, in a manner consistent with the principles of Geneva' (Strasser, p30). Thus these formerly juridical duties of military experience have been turned into the ethical prescriptions of an ambiguously civil life, becoming discretionary and therefore gift-like.

The place evacuated by the language of the law is occupied by the vocabulary of ethics precisely because there exists neither legal obligation nor even a clear doctrine regarding the treatment of detainees. Given this, I suspect it is not incidental that the 'Final report of the independent panel to review Department

---

2. I owe this point to Uday Singh Mehta.

of Defense detention operations' should recommend that all:

> personnel who may be engaged in detention operations, from point of capture to final disposition, should participate in a professional ethics program that would equip them with a sharp moral compass for guidance in situations often riven with conflicting moral obligations (Strasser p99).

Instead of reading the recommendations of the independent panel as a lot of eyewash, or as routine ways of addressing routine military problems, I see them as expressing a genuine attempt to deal with a novel situation - one which includes the troubling insertion into military life of an ambiguously civilian space of ethical rather than juridical existence. 'Some individuals', states the report, 'seized the opportunity provided by this environment to give vent to latent sadistic urges. Moreover, many well-intentioned professionals, attempting to resolve the inherent moral conflict between using harsh techniques to gain information to save lives and treating detainees humanely, found themselves on uncharted ethical ground, with frequently changing guidance from above' (Strasser, p25).

As if to support this position, the 'Investigation of the Abu Ghraib Detention Facility and 205th Military Intelligence Brigade' even quotes Staff Sergeant Ivan L. Frederick II, one of the soldiers accused of the most egregious abuse, telling colleagues who rescued one of his victims: 'I want to thank you guys, because up until a week or two ago, I was a good Christian' (pp167-8). This was well before any photographs had surfaced from Abu Ghraib, or any investigations had been launched.

The emergence of such new spaces within the cultural and institutional life of the armed forces is neither accidental nor unplanned, for the prison we have been looking at in Baghdad marked one site in which the eminently private, civilian and even ethical vision for the military proposed by US Secretary of Defence Donald Rumsfeld achieved its crude beginnings:

> We must transform not only our armed forces but also the Defense Department that serves them - by encouraging a culture of creativity and intelligent risk-taking. We must promote a more entrepreneurial approach: one that encourages people to be proactive, not reactive, and to behave less like bureaucrats and more like venture capitalists; one that does not wait for

threats to emerge and be 'validated' but rather anticipates them before they appear and develops new capacities to dissuade and deter them.[3]

Both the Armed Forces and the State Department had opposed the President's suspension of certain articles in the Geneva Conventions, arguing not only that these were sufficient to deal with the enemy threat, but also that 'to conclude otherwise would be inconsistent with past practice and policy, jeopardize the United States armed forces personnel, and undermine the United States military culture which is based on a strict adherence to the laws of war' (Stresser, p30). Apart from the repercussions of this suspension in terms of international law as well as of international reputation, which were primarily the concerns of the State Department, the military was concerned with the fragmentation of its own culture that such partial suspensions of juridical uniformity represented.

And indeed a whole new world of private or civilian practice soon hove into view, or rather out of view, within the armed forces. For example interrogation techniques as well as moral liberties that had been permissible in Afghanistan and Guantanamo Bay, where the relevant articles of the Geneva Conventions had been suspended, were introduced into Iraq - where they were still in force - through 'a store of common lore and practice within the interrogator community circulating through Guantanamo, Afghanistan and elsewhere' (Stresser, pp34-5).

The juridical fragmentation and privatisation of military life was compounded by its institutional fragmentation and privatisation, given the presence of private contractors or the CIA at a facility like Abu Ghraib, all working under different rules. Naturally the absence of legal or doctrinal uniformity, and the sheer multiplicity of guidance, information and authority present, created areas of confusion, negligence and criminal opportunity in the prison (Stresser, pp73-4). All this would be avoidable if a doctrine governing relations between these various elements was formulated and enforced. What seems to be unavoidable, however, even under the most serene of conditions, is the military's cultural and institutional fragmentation, signalled most disturbingly not by the infiltration of private contractors and the CIA into its domain, but by the spread of private or civilian practices among its own troops.

---

3. Donald H. Rumsfeld, 'Transforming the military', *Foreign Affairs*, Vol. 81, No. 3. May/June 2002, p24.

And this is not a matter merely of temporary exigencies having to do with the particularities of time, place or resources, but apparently marks a new paradigm of war that has emerged since the attacks of 9/11. It is in this light that the deference accorded at Abu Ghraib to non-commissioned officers who had civilian correctional backgrounds becomes significant (Stresser, p81). For no matter how accidental or temporary it might have been, such deferral points to the private, civilian and even ethical nature of new military practices - which, paradoxically, end up treating foreign enemies *like* but not *as* domestic criminals.

Unlike many commentators on the incidents of abuse at Abu Ghraib, who, like those accused of it, blame such incidents on orders given from above, I suspect that American military culture itself had little to do with the sadistic fantasies of the soldiers involved. This is why the two official reports on these episodes are so concerned with the fragmentation of command structures, the private world of unauthorised behaviour and the military risk they represent. Indeed the apparent tolerance of abuse among some of the superiors of those accused, as well as of their colleagues who did not participate in it, poses significant risks to military discipline, as the reports acknowledge by recommending punitive measures and additional training.

The reports also make it very clear that the new paradigm of war announced by the attacks of 9/11, which entailed among other things the suspension of certain among the traditional laws of war, are transforming the American armed forces in an unexpected fashion, by breaking down some of its familiar structures, through, for example, opening it up to multiple sets of rules, as well as to private contractors and other civilians.

What the reports do not mention, however, is the fact that such a breakdown of military structures is only exacerbated by the army's reliance on volunteers who are increasingly being recruited from the margins of American society. The need for such recruits is so great that the armed forces have been compelled to scale back the criminal, psychological and medical criteria by which soldiers were once selected. They also offer recruits more incentives, like higher education and citizenship, thus transforming these men and women into customers who must be catered to in civilian fashion, rather than soldiers controlled by military discipline.[4]

---

4. I owe this point to Neguin Yavari.

A community of spectators

The emergence of the American soldier as a photographer, one who carries a digital camera everywhere, might well play a role in the transformation of the military by way of its infiltration from private and civilian life. These soldiers are as likely to photograph the Commander in Chief on tour - which presents a disconcerting breach in the serried ranks when seen on television - as they are to photograph some instance of abuse.

I n both cases the act of photography breaks up the public and collective identity of the military by introducing within it a strictly private and even civilian desire, since these pictures transform public and professional events into personal ones. One wonders, for example, whether the soldiers at Abu Ghraib had intended to use their cameras as tourists in the friendly Baghdad they expected to encounter, and if the photographs of abuse they ended up taking served also as tourist memorabilia. And what other pictures were taken by these soldiers and stored on the same digital cameras?

The circulation of photographs depicting abuse at Abu Ghraib created a private community of spectators, whose unity was civilian in the sense that it was based on the transgression of military standards as well as of military cohesion, by the sharing of one another's vulnerability in what amounted to the pictorial evidence of individual culpability. The enormous risk of circulating such criminal evidence represents not so much the cockiness or stupidity of those involved as their wilful creation of a community based on trust rather than on rules.

Moreover the sexual fantasies of the American soldiers represented in these photographs, for instance that of a naked man leashed like a dog, are part of popular culture in the United States, and can be found in as mainstream a source as a Madonna music video. These images have little to do with any peculiarity of military life, this I think being part of the problem they pose for the army. Those in the United States who exculpated the soldiers at Abu Ghraib by comparing their actions to hazing rituals at college campuses were not wrong, in the sense that both situations entail the creation of communities that are ethical because based on trust, being in addition part of civilian and private life.

The inverted multiculturalism that apparently made soldiers degrade inmates in specifically 'cultural' ways, such as stripping before women or each other, is also something imported from civilian life - though it serves as a red herring here, disguising the soldiers' own sexual desire in the acting out of standard pornographic roles. It is as if these men and women required the sexual complicity or even participation of their victims, especially by commanding them to masturbate. This form of intimacy, in which American soldiers participated by exposing their own sexual acts to the eyes and ears of Iraqi prisoners, defines Abu Ghraib as a site of ethical practice. For like the relationship of master and slave, that between soldier and prisoner gained its intimacy by losing all regulation.

If slavery sometimes created bonds of passion as much as loyalty between master and servant, intimacy among captors and captives in the War on Terror is also a phenomenon deserving the name of ethics, since it too can lead to a relationship of mutual respect. This is the kind of relationship that we see in places like the US prison at Guantanamo Bay, as well as in the military bases scattered over Afghanistan and Iraq, some of whose soldiers have converted to Islam at the hands of their captives. A more familiar example of this relationship is provided by the so-called Stockholm syndrome, which refers to the sympathy that hostages often develop for their kidnappers. Oddly, these captors are rarely if ever said to participate in the syndrome, being credited only with the sort of imposture and subterfuge that is characteristic of a theatrical villain.

Commanding prisoners to masturbate at Abu Ghraib might well have served as a method to force into being an intimacy that the facility's lack of regulation invited. What does it mean for an inmate to be aroused by such procedures? The consent given to his treatment by the prisoner's arousal works like the videotaped confessions of those who have been captured and executed by insurgents in Iraq. Indeed the circulation of digital photographs and video clips by US military personnel simultaneously with those of Al-Qaeda and other militants, sometimes on the same websites, like ogrish.com, is highly significant. Not only does one set of images often provoke and comment upon the other; each brings into being a secret community by its circulation. And this only fragments and multiplies the war's global audience, for the benefit of which so many of its battles are in fact fought.

I want to bring this set of reflections on Abu Ghraib and the transformation of American military life to a close by pointing to the problem posed by asymmetric warfare to conventional deployments of force. This problem is described very succinctly in the 'Final report of the independent panel to review Department of Defense detention operations', which states that asymmetric warfare 'can be viewed as attempts to circumvent or undermine a superior, conventional strength, while exploiting its weaknesses using methods the superior force can neither defeat nor resort to itself' (Stresser, pp26-7). But though this definition recognises the structural impasse posed by Al-Qaeda, whose organisation, mobility and aims no longer bear much comparison to those of guerrilla or terrorist groups in the past, it does not consider the ways in which such asymmetrical warfare has in fact changed the armed forces.

Does not the collapsing of military distinctions between the external and internal enemy, or the front and rear line, mirror the global jihad's own collapse of the distinction between the near and far enemy, or the military and civilian one? Does not the juridical, cultural and institutional fragmentation of the US armed forces mirror that of Al-Qaeda? And does not diverting military life into private, civilian and even ethical channels mirror a similar diversion in the lives of Islam's holy warriors?

The de-militarisation of the Global War on Terror is partial in nature, but highly significant nevertheless. It provides an important example of the interface between two organisational forms, the hierarchy and the network, that now co-exist at almost every level of social life. Significant about this interface is that it allows the network form to consolidate itself while infiltrating its hierarchical enemy. That the reverse does not occur is crucial, whether or not a particular network - Al-Qaeda in this instance - is eventually demolished. For in the meantime hierarchy has become a kind of monster made up of itself and its opposite.

Zionism, antisemitism and the struggle against racism

Nira Yuval-Davis

Nira Yuval-Davis argues that it is important to distinguish between different histories of racialisation when discussing Zionism as a form of racism.

In spite of the great efforts made by the Israeli government and its supporters throughout the years to keep what has been happening on the ground hidden from the world, the Palestinian issue now occupies the same symbolic space as Apartheid South Africa once did.

In this article I want to revisit a controversial article I published in the feminist newspaper *Spare Rib* more than twenty-five years ago, after Israel invaded Lebanon the first time (which had the same title as this one). That article was an intervention in a conflict between feminists in London at the time. Looking back, I believe that this conflict can be seen as a signpost in the struggle to make a critique of Israel - and of Zionism itself - a legitimate focus for a leftist campaign in Britain.

Experience, identity and race

I had written the piece in response to a controversy over some previous articles - including one by Aliza Cahn, an anti-Zionist Israeli Jew - that had been published by *Spare Rib* (which was at that time the voice of the British feminist movement). These had caused a storm of protest from many Jewish feminists, but the *Spare Rib* editorial collective had decided not to publish any of their letters. Public protest meetings were then called, and there were clashes - mainly between Jewish and black and third world feminists rather than with Palestinian feminists - that involved lots of tears, and at some stages even physical fights. The most extreme mutual denial expressed in these meetings was, on the one hand, a black feminist's claim that only black people could suffer from racism, and that therefore there was no validity for the Jewish women's claims of anti-semitism, and, on the other, a Jewish feminist's statement that, since she lived in London, not Israel, she didn't care what happened in Israel or Lebanon, only about the anti-semitism that she had experienced herself. The Jewish feminists, indignant that *Spare Rib* had constructed the Arabs and Palestinians as the only victims in the Israeli/Arab conflict, and had not given any space to their feelings, ended up collating and publishing their letters in a separate pamphlet.

I had been invited to write an article responding to these issues, but once it was written I had to struggle for nearly a year before the editorial collective approved it for publication. One part of my response was to argue that the insight that the personal is political (a key insight of feminism) had been misused in these debates. 'The personal is political' means that all spheres of personal life, as well as public lives, are political, in the sense that power relations are always present and need to be reflected upon. It does not mean, however, that only personal experience can give us an understanding of the political. On the contrary, interpretations based solely on personal experience - something at times encouraged in the feminist culture of 'consciousness raising' - can lead to both relativist and exclusionary identity politics.

This is not the place to go into a more elaborate critique of identity politics.[1] And in fact, since the heady days of the late 1970s and early 1980s, the more uncritical forms of identity politics, especially among feminists, have largely given way to a more dialogical and encompassing type of politics. Indeed, some of the women involved in the *Spare Rib* protest are now associated with Jews for Justice

---

1. For more on this debate see, for example, my articles 'Identity, Identity Politics and Women', in V.M. Moghadam, *Identity Politics and Women: Cultural Reassertion and Feminism in International Perspective*, 1994; and 'Belonging and the politics of belonging', in *Patterns of Prejudice*, 2006, 40(3).

for Palestinians; and, given the situation of both asylum seekers and Muslims in Britain today, by now there has been an acceptance by many that racism can be directed against groupings that do not have any obvious signifying markers of boundaries - through skin colour, dress, accent and so on - and that it is not directed only against black people.

A critique of identity politics was in fact only a minor part of my article: my main concern was to bring to the feminist audience an alternative understanding of the nature of the Zionist project, as well as the ways it can relate to issues of anti-semitism and racism more generally. (It was my insistence on discussing anti-semitism as well as Zionism that caused the long delay in publishing the article.) It is my view that an understanding of these issues remains vital today - and in some ways even more poignantly.

Settler societies and racialisation

In 1975 - a few years before I wrote the article - the UN passed a controversial resolution to view Zionism as a form of racism;[2] and one of my aims was to show that, although there were many Zionists who were subjectively democratic or socialist - and that throughout Zionist history there had been many voices protesting against some of the unavoidable implications of Zionism in the hope that they were avoidable - Zionism, both as a political movement and as an ideological one, has operated in a racist way. Racism has two ultimate logics - of exclusion, which might end up with extermination - and of exploitation, which might end up with slavery. Different racialisation projects tend to prioritise one logic over the other, but in practice each often brings about the other. In the Zionist case there has been a non-permeable hierarchical and exclusionary boundary between the Jewish and non-Jewish citizens of Israel, which has meant that they generally occupy very specific class positions. This boundary operates in a variety of ways, but its most generalised form before 1967 could be seen in the terms of the Israeli nationality law and the Israeli Law of Return; less explicitly, but more effectively, it also operated through the de facto apartheid system achieved

2. The resolution - number 3379 - was revoked in 1991, after the fall of the Soviet Union; its revoking was one of the conditions made by Israel for participation in the Madrid conference, which officially started what later became known as 'the Oslo process'.

by the double act of the Jewish agency and the Israeli state.[3] After 1967, the Israeli state's occupation of the West Bank and Gaza Strip meant that about a third of the population under its rule were not even formally its citizens: in its post-67 phase a growing list of atrocities and violations of human rights have marked the process of the expansion of the Zionist project.

The UN terminology of Zionism as racism, however, is much too generic to be really helpful in understanding the nature of the Zionist project. There are many different forms of racism and processes of racialisation, and it is necessary to be more specific in looking at any given society. Thus, for example, Israeli society cannot be treated as a multi-cultural racist liberal democracy of the western kind.[4] This was why I was critical of most of the contributors to *The Challenge of Post-Zionism*, which was written during the so-called Oslo Process years: they had bought into one of the great - and most successful - fictions of the Oslo agreement. Fundamentally, the agreement treated Israel and Palestine as two neighbouring states with a border conflict, so that for the conflict to be resolved there was a need to reach agreement on where exactly the border-line should pass, in order to ensure the best security and economic prosperity for both sides. As I pointed out in the conclusion of the book (which I was asked by the editor to write), such an approach mystifies rather than clarifies the issues involved. This is because Israel is not just a multi-cultural racist state; it is a Settler state. Any analysis of the way it operates has to take on board this specific feature of Israeli society.

I first heard the analysis of Israel as a settler state when I attended a *Matzpen* study group on alternative Zionist history in the late 1960s. I also read during that time Maxim Rodinson's book *Israel - a colonial settler state?* (Pathfinder Press 1973), which analysed the Zionist project in a similar way. However, it was not until I visited Australia in the 1980s, and experienced a sense of familiarity, that I fully understood what it actually means for Israel to be a settler society, and how the racialisation processes in Israel are specifically

---

3. The Jewish agency is the operative arm of the Zionist movement; before statehood it was the 'state-on-the-way'; its main aims today are to facilitate the migration of Jews to Israel, to promote Jewish-Zionist education, and to maintain partnership links with the Jewish diaspora.
4. See my (critical) conclusion in Ephraim Nimni (ed), *The Challenge of Post-Zionism*, Zed Books 2002.

those of a settler society. Shortly afterwards I met a colleague from Canada, Daiva Stasiulis, who had had similar insights about Canada when she visited Australia, and we ended up editing a book together, *Unsettling Settler Societies* (Sage 1995), in which we examined ten quite different cases of settler societies, from the USA to Algeria. I co-wrote the chapter on Zionism and Israel with a Palestinian colleague, Nahla Abdo.

In our introduction to the book, Daiva and I defined as settler societies those which were the result of the settlement of European migrant groups in other parts of the world, who were intent on settlement and on building self-sustaining states independent of the metropolitan centre. (We also argued that there is a continuum, rather than a dichotomy, between 'normal' western nation-states and settler societies, because the process of nation building in Europe itself also involved, almost everywhere, settlement by migrant groups, as well as the legal and administrative imposition of the hegemonic centre on the periphery.)

Settler societies are racialised in two very different ways. Firstly, there is the relationship to the indigenous population, which, during the process of settlement, is dispossessed, killed directly or indirectly (for example via the introduction of new diseases against which they have no immunity), and incorporated in a marginal or major way into the economy of the new society. Secondly, however, there is racism against groups of immigrants who are considered necessary for the development of the society, but not as desirable as those from similar racial and ethnic backgrounds to those of the original settlers. In the case of Israel such migrants are represented by the Mizrahi Jews. The settler society, therefore, is very far from being simply a homogenous body of settlers and their descendents. Often one of the ongoing conflicts among anti-racist activists in settler societies stems from a difference between racialised groupings of immigrants, who want to promote a multicultural project in which the indigenous people would be considered as just one more minority community, and the indigenous people themselves, who, even if they constitute only a small number of survivors, reject this approach and insist that the major conflict is between them and what the Australian aboriginals call 'the imposing society'. And indeed, the long-term character of settler societies has always been determined by the ways in which the basic conflicts between the indigenous people and the settlers have been resolved.

Many factors can determine the nature of the resolution - the economic leverage of the indigenous people on the settler society; the nature of the nationalist and civic ideology that has been deployed in the settler society nation-building processes; the number of people of mixed origin in the society; and, of course, more global political and economic factors. I would argue, however, that the most fundamental factor is the demographic relationship between the size of the remaining indigenous population and that of the settlers, once the nation-building process of the settler society has been more or less accomplished. In countries where there is a huge majority of settlers, as in Australia, Canada and the USA, the indigenous people have had to agree to some kind of accommodation that gives them the maximum autonomy and land rights. In cases in which the indigenous people remain a large majority, as in Algeria, Zimbabwe and South Africa, it is the settlers that have to accommodate, at the end of the day - or else leave.

One of the important specificities of the Zionist settler project is that the size of the settler population and that of the indigenous population has been for many years now roughly the same - as a result of various global and local historical circumstances, socioeconomic factors, and cultural and political pressures on women to bear children; but especially because of the operation of demographic policies of ethnic cleansing and migration. This means that no one side is likely to be prepared to concede defeat easily, and that the conflict, other things being equal, will tend to be much longer and bloodier.

Israel's settler history

There are at least two other factors that complicate the Israeli-Palestinian conflict. Firstly, unlike most other settler projects, the Zionist project was autonomous from its inception: it was not an arm of a specific empire, and was constructed as a nationalist project.

During the time of the emergence of the Zionist ideology in central and Eastern Europe, around the time of the dissolution of the Austro-Hungarian and Russian empires, national liberation was perceived to be the solution for many oppressed ethnic minorities. The Jews, however, did not have their own territorial 'homeland' in Europe. The Bund, the other national Jewish movement of that time, sought to solve what was known as 'the Jewish problem' by following Otto Bauer's model. Bauer, an Austro-Hungarian socialist, recognised the ethnic mix of the population in the Austro-Hungarian empire, and the dangers of the impulse of nationalist movements towards territorial homogenisation - or 'cleansing'. He therefore called for the separation of nationality from the state. On the basis of these principles the Bund sought national and cultural autonomy within a future socialist federal state. The Zionist movement, on the other hand (which, unlike the Bund, included both socialists and non-socialists) accepted the 'holy trinity' of nationalist construction - the non-separation of people, state and territory. It therefore looked for a territory in which such a Jewish state could be built. They settled on Palestine because, although it was one of the most developed and densely populated countries of the Middle East, it was the Jewish mythical country of origin as well as the religious 'promised land'.

In many settler society projects, the country is perceived by the settlers as a 'new world' - available not only for immigration but also for establishing a new and better society (often called by Christian religious refugees the 'New Jerusalem'). In the Zionist project, this new society was perceived also to be a rehabilitation of an old one - the biblical Judaic state - and the 'New Jerusalem' was going to be built in the land of 'Old Jerusalem'. Theodor Herzl, the 'father' of the Zionist movement, in his utopian book that was supposed to describe the desired Jewish state, called it 'Altneuland' - the Old/New country. The Zionist movement saw itself as a nationalist movement, but it drew on religious narrative not only for its location of the territorial 'homeland', but also for its constitutive delineating of the boundaries of the nation (although after the holocaust an even more inclusive principle of belonging has come to dominate, i.e. all those who would have been considered as Jews under the Nazi racial laws). Unlike the Bund, who were interested only in Jews who lived in Eastern Europe, the Zionists were interested in Jews from all over the world, in their pursuit of enough bodies for what was known in Australia as the 'populate or perish' drive.

This created a second dimension that is specific to the Israeli Palestinian conflict - one to which not enough attention has been given. While the Arabic national movements imagined a nation (or nations) that would encompass all those who had been living in their territories, as a way of overcoming the religious communal divisions of the Ottoman system, the Zionist movement constructed national boundaries which included people from different territorial origins from all over the world who shared a religious and ethnic origin. The Mizrahi, or Arab Jews, could be defined as belonging within the boundaries according to both of these different principles of construction, but this has not prevented them from ending up as marginal in the one (although by now they constitute the majority of Israeli Jews) and excluded from the other. When I started meeting Arab and Palestinian intellectuals in the late 1960s and early 1970s, they told me that this had been one of the most troubling issues for them, as they felt it was an undermining factor in their fight against religious sectarianism in their own side, which they felt to be one of their most difficult tasks. As we know, this task has proved too difficult. Today, it is not only Jews that are excluded from the Arab nation, but also, progressively, Christians; and inter-sectarian religious wars are becoming more and more central to the politics of the Middle East region

> 'the Zionist movement constructed national boundaries that included people from over all the world who shared a religious and ethnic origin'

as a whole. In Israel, on the other hand, although over the years the influence of political religion has become much more influential, other demographic and political developments have transformed the ultra-orthodox Jews into yet one more fragment of contemporary Israeli society.

F urther useful insights into the nature of Israeli society have been offered in recent years by two other analytical models - the post-colonial divided societies model being developed by Avishai Ehrlich, and the ethnocracy model of Oren Yiftachel.[5] In his comparative research of formerly British-ruled colonial divided societies - in Israel/Palestine, Cyprus, Northern Ireland and especially India/Pakistan - Avishai Ehrlich has pointed to somewhat similar dynamics in all of these societies; religious divisions that have been manipulated during colonialism become principle determinants of national boundary constructions by the conflicting sides, and of their associated ethnic cleansing processes.

Religious differences as signifiers of national boundaries are common also in the ethnocratic regimes that have been the subject of comparative study by Oren Yiftachel. At the time when we started our campaign against the Israeli Law of Return we could argue that there were no other societies that defined

---

5. See Avishai Ehrlich (2004), 'Israel/Palestine and other Divided Societies', paper presented at the conference 'Racisms, Sexisms and Contemporary Politics of Belonging', London, August 2004; Oren Yiftachel, *Ethnocracy: Land and Identity Politics in Israel/Palestine*, University of Penn Press 2006.

themselves as liberal democracies that had this kind of nationality law. Since the fall of the Soviet Union, however, we have seen a speedy growth of such laws in some of the 'post-communist' regimes, for example in Latvia. Ethnocracies, as defined by Yiftachel, are political regimes 'instituted on the basis of *qualified rights to citizenship* and with *ethnic affiliation* as the distinguishing principle, to secure that the most important instruments of state power are controlled on behalf of an ethnic collectivity'. Unfortunately, the 'ethnicisation' of so-called nation-states is on the rise everywhere in the world, partly driven by the pursuit of what Manuel Castells (in *The Power of Identity*, Blackwell 1997) has called 'defensive identity communities' against the effect of neo-liberal globalisation. Ethnic and religious fundamentalist movements have arisen across the world, and the 'clash of civilisations' discourse in the post 9/11 world has given further impetus to the securitisation and militarisation of ethnic, religious and national boundaries.

The role of religion in the Israeli/Palestinian case, however, is even more complex than in most other places, as the Palestinian and Jewish homeland has also been the holy land of Christianity, and is one of the most holy places for Muslims. When one visits the old city of Jerusalem, one can see so many places where ownership has been contested or divided for many hundreds of years - often since the time of the crusades - between different religious denominations. This specific status of the country in the religious discourse of the three monotheistic religions has helped to make it emotionally relevant to - and has sometime even developed a sense of ownership in - millions of people who have never visited the place and have no kinship relationships with the people who live there. Thus many Jews, with the growing hegemony of the Zionist project, have come to see in Israel a post-factum homeland to their diaspora, and even those who remained anti-Zionist on religious grounds, such as the Neturei Karta, feel duty bound to demonstrate against liberal gay laws in Israel as well as in support of the PLO. Muslims all over the world (unlike most Palestinians, however) equate Zionists, Israelis and Jews, and identify the Palestinian resistance as a contemporary struggle of Saladin against the crusaders; and they turn to the Qur'an, as well as to traditional European anti-semitic writings, to support their anti-Jewish views. Christian fundamentalists support Jewish settlements on the West Bank, because, according to their theology, all the Jews need to come back and settle in the holy land: only after that happens will the conditions for the final struggle between light and darkness be fulfilled, after which the Messiah will come back - and then all the Jews who will not convert to Christianity will be killed.

As I argued in the *Spare Rib* article, there is often a relationship between anti-semitism and attitudes towards Zionism and Israel. However, the relationship is not fixed - you can be anti-semitic at the same time as being anti- *or* pro-Zionist (as in the case of the American Christian fundamentalists). And, as I also warned, the insistence of the pro-Israeli lobby on seeing any critique of Israel, let alone Zionism, as anti-semitic, can only end up as a self-fulfilling prophecy. I find it very problematic that even the EU monitoring centre on racism and xenophobia (EUMC) has now accepted as the 'new anti-semitism', 'the vilification of Israel'. As it is so easy to find out about the atrocities that Israel is carrying out against the Palestinians, the equation of critique of Israel with anti-semitism could be seen as a de facto legitimation of anti-semitism, something which in the future could have terrible consequences. We can see the direction in which some of it might be going in Iran's denial of the holocaust (and now they have organised a 'scientific' international conference on the subject), and their call for all Israeli Jews to go to Europe or to Alaska.

There is one further factor that is crucially important for the understanding of the Israeli-Palestinian conflict. The Zionist settler project, since it was not connected to a metropolitan homeland, has always needed to court the dominant global powers in the region - first Britain and then, for most of the time since 1948, the USA. This means that Israel, as part of, and in addition to, pursuing its own interests also serves the interests of the superpower in the area. This might mean exercising military power for them, but it can also sometimes mean - as during the first Gulf War - avoiding the exercise of military power. There are two important consequences of this. Firstly, Israel has an avid interest in the internal politics of the USA, because whoever controls the government there also, to a great extent, controls what Israel is allowed or not allowed to do in pursuit of its own interests. (This political reality explains the great investment of Israel and American Zionists in what is known as the 'pro Israel lobby'. However, any portrayal of Israel as controlling the USA and determining its policies is following in the footsteps of an old anti-semitic stereotype of the Elders of Zion controlling the world.) The second consequence of this positioning of Israel in the Middle East is that it has come to be perceived as the representative of the West. With the rise of capitalism and the destabilisation of Eastern European peasant societies in the second half of the nineteenth century, the Jews were made scapegoats by the peasants, becoming the focus of their hostility towards their rulers, and they suffered from pogroms as a result. Israel is in danger of coming to occupy a parallel role in the contemporary world. The West in general and the USA in particular are losing their ability to rule the rest of the world in a legitimate way, and are, with ever greater frequency, resorting to brute force in order to impose their control - and they frequently fail, as is happening these days in Iraq and Afghanistan, and as happened, mirror-like, when Israel attacked Lebanon and Gaza in summer 2006.

The future

These are very turbulent times, both globally and locally. I can see no easy or near solution to the situation, and I am afraid that in the long run the resolution of the Zionist settler society conflict will be more similar to the Algerian one than to the South African one - and Algeria is not a happy place to live.

When, in the early 1960s, I started to be active in Israel in the struggle for the civil rights of the Palestinian citizens of Israel - who were then under military government, with their lands confiscated because of what was known as 'the Judaization of Galilee' - and then after 1967 against the occupation, I was under the impression that if only we could tell the people in Israel, and then the people in the world, what was really happening there, what had really been happening since the beginning of the Zionist project, we would be able to stop it all. Alas, when we started to be successful and the facts of the occupation - and of Zionist history - started to be better known, things started to get worse, not better. Oscar Wilde once said that hypocrisy is the tribute that vice pays to virtue: once all the facts become exposed, people often stop feeling shame, instead of stopping doing the things that were hidden before. Exposing the reality of the occupation, then, is only a necessary, not a sufficient, condition for bringing positive change about. Removing legitimacy from the state's actions is the next step. Recent attempts to arrest Israeli ministers and military personnel as war criminals when they have travelled overseas are an example of such an activity. All actions that might help to stop the ongoing atrocities carried out by Israel - a rogue and disintegrating state - should be encouraged.

However, things are never that simple. As Nadja al Ali, who is involved in the Iraqi women's organisation Act Together has said in the context of the resistance to the occupation of Iraq, the enemy of my enemy is not necessarily my friend. Unconditional solidarity can only brew troubles for the future. The superficial unconditional solidarity with the Jews after the holocaust served to contribute to the legitimacy of the Zionist project, and continues to this day to paralyse those who see in any critique of Israel or Zionism a form of anti-semitism. We have to avoid repeating this mistake in the contemporary situation.

So what can be the last word in such a situation? I suppose the old Gramscian one, calling on us to keep on with 'pessimism of the mind, optimism of the will'.

This is an edited version of talk first given at SOAS, 7 December 2006.

Is capitalism China's salvation?

Lin Chun

Will Hutton, *The Writing on the Wall: China and the West in the Twenty-first Century*, Little, Brown

Chairman Mao once famously declared, at a time when China was suffering immense rural poverty, that 'only socialism can save China'. Later, due to the Sino-Soviet disputes, the sentiment among many Chinese - however self-deceiving - became 'only China can save socialism'. Furthermore, China's initial market reform project was also firmly socialist in commitment, even though how exactly a market economy might cohere with socialist values was yet to be worked out. And during the optimistic search for a new direction after the cultural revolution, the popularly endorsed ambition - inscribed in the 1978 party resolution - was to build China into a 'highly civilised and highly democratic' socialist society. The debatable meaning of the word at each of these historical moments notwithstanding, 'socialism', as a big idea, has dominated China's ideological discourse and policy considerations for decades. Yet, whilst it walks a different path from the self-dismantling of the Soviet Union and the East-Central European velvet revolutions, the People's Republic has moved just as far away as those other countries from where it all began. More or less lost everywhere in a globalising world, socialism today - even for sympathisers - appears to be no more than day-dreaming, or a euphemism for capitalist transformations. Hence we have Will Hutton's hardly inventive writing on the wall: only capitalism can rescue China from its socioeconomic, environmental and political crises.

Hutton is mostly accurate in his empirical observations on China's structural contradictions and current problems. In particular, he is right to highlight the unsustainability of the country's pattern of development - widely recognised inside China - in terms of its low-wage, low-tech, low-productivity manufacturing at the bottom end of the global supply chain, combined with its high costs of wasteful raw material and energy consumption, heavy pollution, labour exploitation and dependency on foreign trade. Also open to criticism is China's recent, unprincipled participation in global competition for energy resources in Africa and elsewhere. Meanwhile, mounting social discontent and protests are emerging, against a background of widespread incidents of social injustice, rampant corruption, environmental degradation and ethnic/regional imbalances - indicating a profound crisis of legitimacy for the reform regime. And in the larger political context, as Hutton points out, the communist monopoly of power is also responsible for certain institutional weaknesses, such as China's poor legal infrastructure and vulnerable banking system, as well as its repressive approach towards civil liberties and the free flow of information.

What may divide Hutton's readers is not his *evaluation* of these symptoms but his diagnosis and prescription. Hutton's recommendation for the cure of China's contemporary 'Leninist corporatism' is exclusively exogenous. An 'enlightenment agenda', as he phrases it, must be transplanted only from the west. In other words, China has no viable option but to complete the transition it has seemingly begun to capitalism.

To be sure, Hutton's capitalism is carefully qualified, and he distinguishes between different models (of which, beside the Nordic paradise, the US is 'the living embodiment of the links between the Enlightenment and economic growth'), to argue that it should encompass both profit-driven and non-market welfare mechanisms. His ideal is defined by what he sees as constitutive of core Enlightenment values: political and economic pluralism, individual rights and capabilities, and accountability (along with other legitimating norms). Given these qualifications and his perfect awareness of typical paths of state-led capitalist development (both earlier in Europe and later in East Asia) and fine comparative discussions of government functions in China (in both pre- and post-reform periods), the logic of his argument is curious. It is not exactly surprising, but it is still sheer inconsistency that Hutton's panacea for China turns out to be 'genuine wholesale privatisation'. Echoing neoliberal critics inside and outside the country, he is impatient with the mere 'automisation' or 'corporatisation' of state firms; instead, he argues, they should be thoroughly privatised. Ironically, this view confirms rather than challenges the quasi-official ideology currently prevalent among Chinese bureaucrats. For both intellectual and political elites in China, privatisation is seen as the only way out of the growth imperative in general, and problems of collective action in particular.

There are several issues here. What Hutton does not seem to realise is the extent of damage that the private transformation of the state sector has already caused in Chinese economy and society. To name but a few: a huge loss of public wealth, mounting unemployment, intensified inequalities, new urban poverty, the widespread incidence of sweatshops and rocketing industrial accidents, with horrifying human and ecological consequences. Ownership 'clarification' and transfers in China have addressed few of the real problems of state-owned enterprises; instead they have involved disguised forms of robbery of public wealth, while creating serious barriers for much-needed public policy capacity-building. The assumption of the magic of private property is 'verified' by ideology rather than evidence. Furthermore, Hutton is clearly writing within the intellectual canon of liberal capitalism, in which private property is taken as an economic foundation of personal freedom and political democracy. It is hard to believe that he can really be confident that ownership and citizenship will 'go hand in hand'. Are we back to the propertied franchise of pre-modern ages? And what about greed, fear, alienation and destruction - hidden or open - in the everyday experience of the marketplace?

Hutton's ideal situation is of course not class polarisation but popular stock holding. Yet even if (and it is a big if) the latter could indeed be achieved through privatising state sectors, it remains obscure as to whether, and why in principle, private ownership is desirable. What proves or justifies this supposed desirability? The enduring power of the belief in the west in the virtue, supremacy and necessity of property is extraordinary in the light of its relatively narrow historical origin, and the far-reaching and perpetual oppositions it has produced. Though its manifestation in the multiple trajectories of different western societies remains itself problematic, the case for private property is freely forced upon other conditions and cultures, among which there are some that are very little affected by a Roman law preoccupation with the possessive individual. As ample studies in moral economy and anthropology demonstrate, individualistic and possessive views of personhood are not necessarily appealing everywhere, and there is no intrinsic ethical value to possessive individualism. Even within Europe, divergences between the English common law tradition and the continental systems in their attitudes toward property are quite notable.

Lamenting the American retreat from Enlightenment values, Hutton nevertheless romanticises capitalism. He is utterly uncritical of key factors in the reality of capitalist globalisation. One may ask, for example, whether the US economy would survive just as well without the unique and decisive advantages it enjoys, such as its military might and dollar hegemony. Equally, the disasters of third world capitalism in the wake of colonial and imperialist devastation and exploitation find no room in his rosy picture. This oversight is relevant because clearly, in various forms, such history continues. China's WTO membership has helped accelerate the country's volume of foreign trade, while costing its cotton and soybean producers and textile exporters dearly - thanks to ruthless competition under rich nations' trade rules, from their subsidies of agricultural exports to targeted anti-dumping laws and tariffs. Labour standards are often used to justify 'punishment' of China, yet China's 2006 draft Labour Contract Law was fiercely resisted by global corporate lobbying. The American and EU Chambers of Commerce and the US-China Business Council objected to almost all the proposed provisions for Chinese workers. They threatened to withdraw investment and move to other places where labour would be cheaper and less demanding. It sounds as though Enlightenment values are not applicable to China (as they were not for the old colonies), *not* because the Chinese reject them, but because multinational businesses block these values wherever they go outside the capitalist heartland.

Hutton confines his discussion of non-market welfarism to post-Enlightenment development in the west, thereby neglecting the vast, and independent, existence of comparable practices in other regions long before and after the European Enlightenment. The ancient Chinese notion of *Datong* or great harmony, which promotes universal wellbeing as a natural right and social duty, is 3000 years old. It has nothing to do with events in Europe, yet resembles a European ideal of rational humanism. China's post-revolutionary efforts in meeting basic needs are an even stronger instance of the ways in which local sources of social development have been mingled with ideas of a western origin (above all, Marxism). Further examples are numerous throughout Asia, Latin America and Africa. Needless to say, as many accounts have demonstrated, the Enlightenment (or plural Enlightenments) attained a substantial degree of its 'universality' by absorbing wisdoms and innovations from various non-European civilisations.

Many of Hutton's critiques and suggestions on China are well made, and would be shared by 'native' Chinese voices. However, because of his bias towards capitalist norms and western sources of normative values, he has missed many of the most popular and engaged debates on the ground. He pays no attention, for example, to the controversy over government failures in ensuring the legality, fairness and transparency of industrial restructuring - or, even more tellingly, to the arguments over the ideology of privatisation itself. Nor does he notice the related legislative struggle over the drafting of China's first property law. (Before its adoption in April 2007, the provisional law, first submitted to the National People's Congress in 2002, had been through extensive public readings and was repeatedly rejected under massive pressure to protect certain state assets and provision.) Obviously, such exercises of participation and deliberation are extremely important in a political system badly needing democratic reforms.

Judging from the deepening and expansion of social activities and movements like these, future possibilities in China may lie well beyond Hutton's ready-made scheme. Abandoning conventional versions of developmentalism - capitalist and socialist alike - there has been a collective search for an alternative. Consider the construction, in the past twenty years or so, of productive, commercial and service centres as townships in the vast rural areas, which defy the paradigmatic route of modernisation (through industrialisation-induced urbanisation). Consider also the recent undertaking to rebuild a universal medical care system throughout urban and rural China, which resumes a lost strategic focus on human and social development. Consider further the green GDP package among other recent proposals by government and non-governmental pressure groups alike, for a new social order that would prize direct producers and stimulate beneficial policies for small businesses and locally-rooted cooperatives. A need-driven, energy-efficient, low-carbon and eco-social friendly economy, superior to private systems of overproduction and overconsumption, is believed to be attainable in China. If the country is to stand a chance it will have to build on its indigenous traditions, from *Datong* to socialist self-reliance and communal organisation. Stressing local knowledge and ethos is therefore a political not cultural, argument. With a little bit more sympathy and a little bit less prejudice, Hutton might even be able to spot some affinities or convergences between elements of socialist struggle in China and those of a European social model in the making.

The point at issue is therefore the politics of legitimation - or what Hutton terms 'justification' - rather than an argument about 'diversity'. For Hutton, justification for one idea or cluster of ideas is seen as an exclusive process, which seeks to delegitimise other, competing, ideas; indeed the process of justification often depends on the delegitimising of other options. And this is where Hutton is ultimately unconvincing, as such a process eliminates potentially valuable alternatives. 'Our concern in the west', he declares (with me doing a slight decoding in brackets), 'should be to help China face its enormous challenges, without damaging us in the process. If Chinese communism can transform itself [on our terms], then China could, like Japan before it, smoothly integrate into the world power system [dominated by us]. If not, severe convulsions lie ahead'. Moreover, 'the increasing presence of China, along with India, Brazil and Russia, will destabilise the global system' - as though that system *is* stable, and as though it is *so* perfect that the rise of developing worlds would not be a good thing for movement towards a more equal and just global order. Finally, in a no doubt well-intended-sentence, Hutton lays his neo-imperialist ideology bare: 'The West needs to stand by its values and institutions at home, and reproduce them internationally to give the rest of the world a genuine opportunity to catch up and to recast its domestic organisation around Enlightenment principles'.

The tone is all too familiar; and by the same token all too disappointing: a commentator as knowledgeable as Will Hutton ought to display a finer judgement. *The Writing on the Wall* is a timely and important book, and immensely stimulating. Its conclusions, however, are too easy. Existing capitalism is no salvation for China. Nor can it save the world from its multiple and chronic crises. There *is* not writing on the wall - the very logic and rules of global capitalist development itself need to be subject to critical scrutiny and creative resistance.

Liberalism in Iran

Iranian philosopher
Ramin Jahanbegloo
in conversation with
Danny Postel

Ramin Jahanbegloo is one of Iran's preeminent intellectual figures and in this role has been responsible for bringing Indian, European and North American intellectuals to lecture there, acting as a kind of philosophical ambassador between Iran and the outside world. This is an edited version of an email correspondence between Jahanbegloo and Danny Postel. In April 2006, Jahanbegloo was arrested and placed in solitary confinement in Tehran's notorious Evin prison for four months. Without bringing any formal charges against him, the regime floated vague accusations of 'contacts with foreigners' and fomenting a 'soft' or 'Velvet' revolution. As a condition of his release, he was required to make a degrading 'confession' of his 'crimes'. Now out on bail, he awaits trial. For further information see www.macleans.ca/ramin.

You've talked about a 'renaissance of liberalism' taking place in Iran. Where does liberalism stand in Iranian intellectual and political life today?

Sartre starts his essay 'The Republic of Silence' in a very provocative manner, saying, 'We were never more free than under the German occupation'. By this Sartre understands that each gesture had the weight of a commitment during the Vichy period in France. I always repeat this phrase in relation to Iran. It sounds very paradoxical, but - 'We have never been more free than under the Islamic Republic'. By this I mean that the day Iran is democratic, Iranian intellectuals will put less effort into struggling for the idea of democracy and for liberal values.

In Iran the rise of hedonist and consumerist individualism, spurred by the pace of instrumental modernisation after the 1979 Revolution, has not been accompanied by a wave of liberal measures. In the early days of the Revolution liberals were attacked by Islamic as well as leftist groups as dangerous enemies and betrayers of the Revolution. Then the American hostage crisis effectively sounded the death knell for the project of liberalism in Iran.[1] But in recent years, with the empowerment of Iranian civil society and the rise of a new generation of post-revolutionary intellectuals, liberal ideas have found a new vibrant life among many intellectuals and students.

The ideas and sensibilities that comprise contemporary Iranian liberalism were more or less formulated by intellectuals such as Muhammad Ali Furughi a century ago. But liberalism is perceived by its contemporary supporters as a more critical project than it was in Furughi's time. In the 1920s and 1930s, liberalism was a technique of progress, something to be activated as a universally executable programme, irrespective of the local contours of culture. It was regarded as a system of protocols that, when enacted by policy-makers, ensured the creation of institutions that enshrined the rule of law, and generated a rationally organised and governed public life. But the species of liberalism which has taken hold today, though it is complementary with the traditional wave of liberalism in Iran, is decidedly original.

Thanks to the recent translations of liberals dominant in the Anglo-American world, such as Isaiah Berlin, John Rawls and Karl Popper, and an appreciation of older traditions of liberalism (from Kant, Mill or Locke), a new trend of liberalism has taken shape among the younger generation of Iranian intellectuals. Their view of a liberal society is related to a view of humanity and truth as inherently unfinished, incomplete, and self-transforming. The principles of Iranian liberalism cannot be grounded in religious truth, because the very idea of free agency, as it is understood today by Iranian liberals, goes

---

1. Sixty-six Americans were taken hostage by Muslim students and held in the American embassy in Tehran between November 1979 and January 1981 (for 444 days in total). An attempt at military rescue ordered by Democratic President Jimmy Carter failed, and possibly scuppered the Democrats in the 1980 American presidential election.

against any form of determinism (religious or historical).

In a country like Iran, where the logic of the theological-political is still absolute, and where there is a single master-value, the principal goal of liberals is to fight for the idea of value-incommensurability, the idea that there are different values which come from different properties and ... to affirm a pluralism of ethical values and different modes of being. Strategically, the chief task of Iranian liberalism is to establish the proper balance between critical rationality and political decency. A lack of liberalism, symbolised by the rise of unreasonable and violent radicalism in the Iranian Revolution (both on the left and the right), has committed a huge injury to our common-sense ways of political thought and political action, and led to deep confusion about questions of moral responsibility and collective human solidarity based on individual self-creation.

In more concrete terms, against the revolutionary model of citizenship a new model of citizenship is suggested by Iranian liberals who work as human rights activists, NGO organisers, intellectuals and students - a model defined in terms of the empowerment of Iranian civil society; the expansion of human solidarity; privately pursued projects of self-creation; moral education of the public; and the development of the vocabulary of liberal democracy. The insistence of Iranian liberals on the concept of 'civil society' as a space which stands in necessary opposition to the state is a check on the arbitrary and authoritarian tendencies in Iranian society. The creation of many voluntary associations, independent journals and reviews and social and cultural NGOs - a genuinely participatory arena of civic engagement and deliberation - has played a crucial role in the promotion of civil society in Iran. As such Iranian civil society remains an important site of dissent and a battleground for liberals who try to bridge the gap between the formal structures of democratic governance and the cultural, social and economic conditions for the realisation of democracy in Iran.

Can you talk about Jurgen Habermas's visit to Tehran in 2002 and the effect it has had on the Iranian intellectual scene?

Habermas's visit to Iran was a huge success. He was treated in Iran the way Bollywood actors are treated in India. Wherever he went or lectured, he was encircled by hundreds of young students and curious observers. (This same phenomenon happened when Richard Rorty visited Iran in 2004: around 1500 souls came to his lecture on 'Democracy and Non-Foundationalism' at the House of Artists in Tehran.) Habermas's visit to Iran was an important event in the process of democratic thinking and dialogue among cultures. The time of philosophical ideas has come in Iran; philosophy represents a window on Western culture, on an open society and on the idea of democracy. This is the reason why Habermas, Rorty, Ricoeur, Berlin and many others are relevant. Most intellectuals in Iran today are struggling against different forms of fundamentalism, fanaticism and orthodoxy.

Habermas is considered the inheritor of the Frankfurt School's intellectual tradition, which from the very beginning questioned all orthodoxies and authoritarianisms. Figures such as Adorno, Horkheimer, Marcuse, Fromm and Benjamin are all very well known in Iran. Those who are interested in Critical Theory focus a great deal on the works of these thinkers and there is a network of readers of the Frankfurt School. And I think there is another reason why Habermas is so popular in Iran. It has to do with the failure of Marxist-Leninist movements in Iran and a new interest in Marx and Hegel. A younger generation of intellectuals and scholars is interested in rediscovering these thinkers, and Habermas sees himself as a nexus in which Marxist thought is reformed, refined, and brought forth to a new generation. Habermas's theory of communicative action derives largely from Marx but involves a systematic rethinking of Marx's ideas. Last, but not least, I think that Habermas's positive assessment of the Enlightenment and his insistence on its democratic potential finds its true place in the lively debate between the two concepts of tradition and modernity in contemporary Iran. What interests many Iranian intellectuals in Habermas's philosophy is his notion of 'theoretical enlightenment' and the possibility of translating it into practical enlightenment. Habermas's advocacy of what he calls post-metaphysical thinking is of great relevance to Iranian intellectuals today.

I think Habermas sheds new light on the problem of democratic agency through a new reading of Kant, Hegel, Marx and Weber. His discourse theory appropriates the Hegelian theme of 'recognition' and takes it a step further. Mutual recognition, understood as the mutual recognition of each other as free individuals, is a minimal condition in the Hegelian as well as in the Habermasian theme of recognition.

This brings me to Kant. Kant is a very popular philosopher in Iran and there were several celebrations in Tehran for the bicentenary of his death in 2004. Once again, Habermas's recasting of the Kantian principle of autonomy and its political implications shows how public reason lies at the heart of democratising processes, and is decisive to the survival of non-authoritarian political, social, and economic institutions. Habermas via Kant offers Iranian intellectuals and civil society activists a model of democratic agency and political thinking that avoids two unattractive alternatives: that of rooting politics in personal preferences for authoritarian personalities and that of eliminating the universality of ethics in the name of a revolutionary break.

Hannah Arendt is also quite popular in Iran today. What can you tell us about this?

Arendt's ideas have been not only closely studied but also acutely felt by many Iranian scholars. I believe that Arendt's popularity in Iran after the Revolution of 1979 is due to the fact that many among us saw a similarity between our experience of living with political violence and totalitarian ideologies (whether Islamist or Marxist-Leninist) and her own alienating political experience as a Jewish refugee who was excluded from participating in public life. This is the main reason why the first translation of Arendt published in Iran was *The Origins of Totalitarianism*. Many Iranians had no idea in 1979 what a totalitarian state was, because most of us were in no way affected by the experience of Nazism or Communism. Actually for a long time the Iranian left dismissed the claim that communism in the Soviet Union and Eastern Europe were forms of totalitarianism.

I think Arendt's work on totalitarianism is key to showing us that evil is an important problem in everyday politics, and that it has the possibility to emerge at any time and in any place. I believe that many have experienced in Iran what Arendt describes in the *Origins of Totalitarianism* as 'the anti-political principle' - the extirpation of ethics in the political realm and the unlimited degradation of civic morality. In 1979 the abyss between men of civility and men of brutal deeds was filled in Iran with the ideologisation of the public sphere. One saw the breakdown of the old system, followed by the failure of political liberalism and the formation of the ideologies of 1979. One can say that when common sense breaks down or becomes impossible, hopelessness and resignation set in; people lose the capacity for action and despair over their ability to influence things.

Why, in your view, are Iranian intellectuals and students generally not attracted to Marxist thinkers and ideas? Why do you think they tend not to be engaged by political currents like the anti-globalisation movement or anti-imperialism?

In Iran the number of 'Marxists' was always a hundred times greater than the number of people who had actually read and studied Marx. This is the main reason why Iranian Marxism had so much trouble making sense of the Iranian Revolution. The Tudeh Party (Iranian Communist Party) and leftist groups in Iran have no explanation today for their political and ideological struggles against liberal and democratic ideas. Most of these Marxist groups supported the anti-democratic measures taken against women and liberals. Most of them also supported the hostage-taking at the American embassy. Some of them even backed the hard-line clerics in the elections and contributed to the Bolshevik idea of leadership by a select few.

Now, I ask you the question: what do you think is left of the left in Iran? Nothing! Some live in exile around the world. Some are doing business in Iran. Some have become collaborators. A few are good scholars who teach in American and Canadian universities. Many lost their lives and will never be back among us. I salute their courage, even if I think that they were totally wrong in what they did. But those Iranian Marxist-Leninists who continue to follow their traditional line of thinking have become an anthropological curiosity: after all their political and intellectual failures, they continue to regard their point of view as a privileged theory, because they believe that it represents the point of view of the proletariat and the proletariat is the class which realises the passage to the true history of humanity.

There are two problems here: first, no vision of history, even if it represents the view of 'the last class of history', can bring an end to all action and discussion on and in history. Second, there is really no organised proletariat in Iran, and the action and self-awareness of the working class in 1979 did not take shape in the direction of a socialist revolution. On the contrary, it was clearly in favour of the Islamic revolution. The heyday of Marxist intellectuals in Iran was over as soon as the Islamic nomenclature was firmly entrenched in power. And despite the great extent of its earlier influence, Iranian Marxism was not successful in the realm of intellectual achievements

During the Pahlavi era, Marxism was propagated by the upper middle class, who were politically against the regime, and the most prepared intellectually to embrace new ideas. Marxism provided them with an intellectual grounding for a rupture with Islamic traditions. But, despite this vibrant interest in Marxist ideas, if you looked at the writings of the Marxist groups you would be horrified by their low level of philosophical knowledge and by their Stalinist tone and content. Most members of the Iranian Communist Party considered Stalin a great hero (and some continue to do so). Their most important deficiency was a lack of awareness about the force of religion and the strong social networking of the Islamist groups in Iran. They lacked an appreciation of Islam as an important social-historical factor in the formation and consolidation of the Iranian masses. Despite their ambition to be close to the masses, they never spoke the language of common people; they were hopelessly out of tune with their own traditions and idioms.

The methodological position of the new generation of Iranian intellectuals is in direct opposition to this tradition of Iranian Marxism. It is characterised by two attitudes: the extension of anti-utopian thinking and the urge for dialogue with the modern West. New thinking in Iran rejects any given consensus as a foundation, whether traditional authority or a modern ideology. And it calls for an institutionalisation of public debate in the form of rational argumentation. The real dividing line between the generations runs between the preachers of grand narratives and monistic utopias and the admirers of dialogue and pluralism of values. In short, what all this means is that the new Iranian intellectual has finally returned to earth, to the here and now, after decades of ideological temptation and looking for salvation in eschatological constructions.

Concerning anti-globalisation movements in Iran - as elsewhere, anti-capitalism has turned into anti-globalisation among left-wing groups. Most of the anti-globalisation groups in Iran are those who mourn the downfall of the Soviet Union as a countervailing superpower, but you also find critics of globalisation among the Islamic groups close to the government. This has to do with the fact that the main source of anti-globalisation sentiment is resentment of US military and economic hegemony. There is also a third group of young intellectuals who seem to be very much influenced by the works of Derrida, Foucault, Agamben, Badiou and Zizek. Their influence often takes nihilistic overtones. On the other hand, you can find some democratic universalists and cosmopolitan intellectuals in Iran, like myself, who do believe that, since globalisation will not ensure the advancement of positive social agendas, we need to empower civil society in the domestic sphere, as it represents a countervailing power and prospects for better governance.

You mentioned the urge in Iran for what you call a 'non-imitative dialogue' with the modern West. Can you explain what this means?

In my debates with Richard Rorty I have suggested a distinction between two concepts of 'universalism': a 'soft' universalism and a 'hard' universalism. 'Soft' universalism provides us with a theoretical framework for various possible versions of moral life, without being founded in a fixed idea of the self. Soft universalism does not force us to make one choice, but offers us reasons and arguments for principles that we might adapt. In other words, soft universalism acknowledges the universal right to reciprocity in a world of plural values, in order to allow people with different values to accept one another. In contrast, 'hard' universalism is in search of uniformity, because it does not accept the principle of cultural pluralism.

For many the paradox of the human rights corpus is that it seeks to foster diversity and difference, but does so only under the rubric of Western democracy: diversity is good so long as it is exercised within the Western paradigm of liberalism. As a result, the centre of the debate turns on the argument over whether or not Western democracy should be considered as a universal principle. Today Western democracy is challenged by religious fundamentalists, and by nihilistic groups, on the grounds that it represents a form of political imperialism or hegemony. Well, I believe that, even if democracy is not as easily spread or as deeply rooted as many American thinkers and politicians have assumed, there is no shadow of doubt but that each democratic process is a potential ally in the struggle against the challenges of our century - such as ethnic and religious conflicts, terrorism, poverty and environmental degradation. This is why I think that the idea of 'democratic universalism' could be the best way of having a non-hegemonic implementation of human rights in countries where individual freedom is not fairly distributed.

This goes hand in hand with the idea of a 'non-imitative dialogical exchange', through which I suggest an intellectual discourse for redefining communities and individual-community relationships in a pluralistic way. I also refer here to the concept of 'transculturation' - which is very different from 'acculturation'.[2] Transculturation involves entering and living in another culture without necessarily appropriating its mode of being. Transculturation is the inclusion of new elements in an existing culture. It is the ability to grasp other traditions and to incorporate them into one's own system of thought.

D ealing with modernity in a dialogical way means having the right to speak back to it. And this response becomes, in effect, a part of the process of modernity itself. A dialogical engagement is an open-ended process where the meaning is situated in the *relation* of the cultural subjects who are in dialogue; they add to each other's identity through the exchange. A dialogue among cultures is the only way in which our ignorance of other cultures and civilisations can be aired, our biases challenged, and our knowledge expanded. We are talking here about an exchange between conscious partners based on a respectful confrontation of their experiences and the knowledge of the process.

There is no imitation in such interactions. My argument is that countries like Iran, Turkey and Egypt have imitated modernity for a long period of time instead of having a critical exchange with it. The result of this uncritical exchange with modernity has been a total subjection to different modes of instrumental rationality, with no emphasis on the critical driving forces of modernity - which are, in Kantian terms, 'escape from tutelage' and 'public use of reason'. Modernity is fundamentally about the reflexive making of history, and in this process the struggle for mutual recognition occupies the most important place. This struggle for mutual recognition arises from dialogue: a mutual desire for respect. We have to look for a universalism which is founded on all human experiences of history rather than only on Western values. This is only possible through large-scale cultural encounters. Taking into consideration the ontological impact of these encounters, an outsider's judgement and discussion of local violations of human rights cannot be criticised as unwarranted ideological interference.

You were in debate with Richard Rorty at Tehran's House of Artists. What was the debate about?

---

2. As expressed in Tzvetan Todorov's *The Conquest of America: The Question of the Other*, Harper and Row 1984.

According to Rorty the golden age of bourgeois liberal democracy is now coming to an end. It lasted two hundred years, and it was good while it lasted, but we can no longer afford it. People are nowadays being easily persuaded to surrender their freedoms in the interests of 'homeland security'. Unlike previous liberal thinkers, Rorty insists that liberal democracy can get along without philosophical presuppositions, and that democracies are now in a position to throw away the ladders used to construct them. Rorty came back to his idea that an attempt to ground democracy in philosophical principles is futile because it would be couched in an obsolete and naive philosophical paradigm. In line with his anti-foundationalism, he argued that there is no way to reconcile universal and particular epistemological justifications. He directed our attention to the manner in which an anti-foundationalist position can yield ethical claims. Anticipating charges of cultural relativism, Rorty came back to his ideas on 'human rights culture' and maintained that the claim that human rights are morally superior does not have to be backed by positing universal human attributes.

In my reply, I tried to show that Rorty's light regard for the political and lack of interest in the institutional conditions for realising ethical ideals could present problems in any exchange on human rights. For many people in non-Western countries, the human rights corpus, as a philosophy that seeks the diffusion of democracy and its primary urgency around the globe can, ironically, be seen as favourable to political and cultural homogenisation and hostile to difference and diversity. As a result of this point of view, you can find many Iranian or Indian intellectuals who see universalism as the product of European history and challenge it as a form of political imperialism.

As a non-Western intellectual who believes firmly in the ideas of democracy and human rights, I have been uneasy with the way Rorty seems to put discussion of the political on hold. I see 'soft' universalism as the only hope for promoting democracy in non-democratic cultures. I believe that his take on the desirability of human rights free of claims to their naturalness is an open-ended debate. But it certainly requires a long process of political and cultural argumentation and persuasion, one which many non-democratic societies, like ours, cannot afford for the time being.

Is there interest in Noam Chomsky and Edward Said in Iran today?

Both Edward Said and Noam Chomsky are very well known in Iran and some of their books have been translated into Persian. They are respected among Iranian intellectuals mainly because of their struggle against extremism and authoritarianism. I think that Said and Chomsky are also important to us because their intellectual task has been a perpetual struggle against the negative role played by the media in sidelining and covering up, if not altogether eliminating, 'undesirable' news. Said and Chomsky represent intellectual integrity and responsibility. Their continuous struggle and hard work is a testimony to the role of the intellectual in today's world and the intellectual's position as an 'outsider', and the role of a critical traveller of cultures and traditions in the age of the global village. Few figures have been able to bring together the radical denunciation of cultural and political hegemony with such a deeply felt commitment to democratic universalism as Said and Chomsky.

I want to focus for a moment on the political content of their ideas. You've painted a picture of a liberal renaissance in Iran today, in which the language of democracy, rights, and pluralism has a deeper resonance than does the language of anti-imperialism, anti-globalisation, and anti-capitalism. Although you're certainly right to emphasise the universalism and humanism of both Chomsky and Said, there's no avoiding the fact that the central issue around which their political writings revolve is that of imperialism. Anti-imperialism is not the animating spirit or the central issue for Iranian liberals, whereas anti-imperialist and Third Worldist motifs formed the core of the Iranian Marxist paradigm, which - as you pointed out earlier - was a failed project that the younger generation of Iranian intellectuals largely rejects. Is there not a tension or disjuncture here, between the liberal-democratic-pluralist project and the radical anti-imperialist one?

One can be a liberal and be anti-imperialist. As you know, there is a tradition of anti-imperialist liberals in the West. One can talk about an anti-imperialist liberal tradition in the West, even if it was weak in its institutional continuity in a country like the United States. (And if we turn to contemporary Iranian history, in blocking liberal, secular nationalism in 1953, the Americans unwittingly played an important role in ensuring the rise of Islamic fundamentalism in that country a quarter of a century later.)

I situate myself on the side of people like Said and Chomsky, as someone who stands at a distance from a tradition, in order to be able to develop his critical capacities in regard to that tradition. I think Empire is not merely a political relationship of power and domination, but revolves around the power to control the other's state of mind. Therefore, the job of a critical intellectual is neither to accept the dominion of another culture, nor to get swallowed by a nativist politics of identity which ends up with a culturally relativist or fundamentalist attitude. But fighting for democracy and values such as pluralism in a country like Iran or Iraq does not necessarily mean accepting the American way of life. Arabs, Turks, Iranians, Indians and many others are no longer living on the 'periphery' of history, because there is no longer any one centre anywhere; we have all become centres.

Although you, Ramin, value and derive insight from the work of both liberal-pluralist thinkers like Berlin and radical anti-imperialist thinkers like Said and Chomsky, are Said and Chomsky as popular among Iranians today - young Iranians in particular - as are Berlin and Habermas?

I am always amazed to see the level of interest of Iranian youth in philosophy. I think this is because philosophy is experienced as a mode of resistance against political ideologies and religious dogmatism. So no wonder Berlin, Habermas, Rorty, Foucault, Derrida, Ricoeur and others are far more popular than Chomsky.

There are many who argue that western 'outsiders' should stay out of Iran's issues, but Shirin Ebadi rejected this position.[3] She said: 'All defenders of human rights are members of a single family ...When we help one another we're stronger.'

I fully agree with Shirin Ebadi on this issue. Since the idea of human rights transcends local legislation and the citizenship of the individual, support for human rights can come from anyone - whether or not she is a citizen of the same country as the individual whose rights are threatened. A foreigner does not need the permission of a repressive government to try to help a person whose liberties are being violated. I am a human rights universalist, but I do not think

---

3   Shirin Ebadi is a lawyer and human rights activist, and was awarded the Nobel peace prize in 2003.

that one can enforce human rights and liberal values through violence or military force. I am, however, for humanitarian intervention, as it is practised by human rights activists and NGOs around the world. Human rights provide us with a standard of conduct which no one can now ignore. Human rights are primary core values of human civilisation. They are far from being perfect, but they are the cornerstones of our daily struggle for human dignity around the world.

Thanks to Logos journal of modern society and culture (www.logosjournal.com) for permission to reproduce an edited version of this correspondence. To read it in full see www.logosjournal.com/issue_5.2/jahanbegloo_interview.htm

Britain's Longest Running Anti Militarist Newspaper

celebrating 71 years of radical publishing

Established in 1936, *Peace News* has been the voice of the British peace movement since its inception. Written and produced by activists, campaigners and radical academics *Peace News* brings you a mix of news and comment that you simply won't find anywhere else.

Founded on the core values of radical pacifism, empowerment and non-violent direct action, we stand shoulder to shoulder with all those struggling to make this a better, safer world to live in. By subscribing to *Peace News* you are ensuring that this unique voice for radical nonviolence can prosper - its a voice that's never been more needed.

To get your monthly copy of Peace News call 0845 456 5183 or visit the website

www.peacenews.info

WAR . PEACE . CLIMATE . TRADE . NUKES . LIBERTIES
NEWS . VIEWS . IDEAS . EVENTS . ACTION . COMMUNITY . CHANGE

Three poems

A desire in the bangles

A desire is in the girl's bangles:
first they will break on his bed
then on the threshold of his house.
But why on the threshold?
Because in the girl there is a woman
mourning - who is not yet
a widow
but a widow to be.
The girl's fear throbs in her veins
as far as her bangles
The girl's desire throbs in them
The girl's mourning throbs in them
Mourning?
Where is the girl's man
for whom mourning runs in her veins
for whom desire is in her bangles?
Her man is caught
in some other body
some other dream
sorrow, other tears

His every sorrow, dream, tear
is beyond the reach of the mourning girl...
But the girl is only a girl
in her is that primal innocence,
madness, death,
whose punishment
she will give to that man
one day
when she will break her bangles...[1]

Gagan Gill
Translation by Jane Duran and Lucy Rosenstein
(Poetry Translation Centre)

---

1. A Hindu woman wears glass bangles as a sign of marriage and must break these when she becomes a widow.

Anthropological account

This is a long distance field trip
to frozen, slippery mountain tops
frozen reefs which have surfaced slowly
silently, of their own accord;
the friction of frozen waves' rigid planes
the only sound in a clean, white, unearthly panorama.
My presence is merely a breath in the solitude.

Strangely, thin, clear clouds and mist
feed nostalgia for the earth's warmth.
Is this all that's left of the feast of colours I know?
Nine suns radiate, eight moons' glowing circles
and the turbulence of stratospheric waves,
reddish purple.

What is left of the wind's quiet swish
preserving the sound - your faint call, perhaps
from behind this reef, now starting to drift away?
Earlier, these two frozen mountains almost collided
but in the end didn't even touch.
Now they will sink, albeit slowly,
swallowed by a slow-moving current
- the dream dance of approaching death -
foundering in the deepest sea.

Who brought me here?
Where - who - am I?

There is an alcove in the building where we sit
separated only by a pile of books.
There is a bench on the front porch and - heavens! -
you freely grope between my thighs.
There is a shady tree in the courtyard and
to the amusement of our friends
we exchange love letters.

Now, just breath, and nostalgia without memory,
the affliction of amnesia, bitter and painful.
Early dawn, three in the morning,
catastrophe that doesn't make the news.
I am woken by sobs.

In my dream, fingers were wiping my cheeks.
The snow of Antarctica? Or frozen tears?

I remember reading in a monograph
that the Inuit take their old people
to a remote place for a final time
and leave them there
for the ice and snow
to release them.

Toeti Heraty
Translated by Carole Satyamurti
(SOAS Poetry Translation Centre)

America, America

God save America
My home sweet home!

The French general who raised his tricolour
over Nagrat al-Salman where I was a prisoner thirty years ago …
in the middle of that U-turn
that split the back of the Iraqi army,
the general who loved St Emilion wines
called Nagrat al-Salman a fort …
Of the surface of the earth, generals know only two dimensions:
whatever rises is a fort
whatever spreads is a battlefield.
How ignorant the general was!
But *Liberation* was better versed in topography.
The Iraqi boy who conquered her front page
sat carbonised behind a steering wheel
on the Kuwait-Safwan highway
while television cameras
(the booty of the defeated and their identity)
were safe in the truck like a storefront
on rue Rivoli.
The neutron bomb is highly intelligent,
it distinguishes between
an 'I' and an 'Identity'.

God save America
My home sweet home!

Blues

How long must I walk to Sacramento
How long will I walk to reach my home
How long will I walk to reach my girl
How long must I walk to Sacramento
For two days, no boat has sailed this stream
two days, two days, two days
Honey, how can I ride?
I know this stream
but, O but, O but, for two days
no boat has sailed this stream

La L La La L La
La L La La L La
A stranger gets scared
Don't fear dear horse
Don't fear the wolves of the wild
Don't fear for the land is my land
La L La La L La
La L La La L La
A stranger gets scared

God save America
My home sweet home!

I too love jeans and jazz and *Treasure Island*
and Long John Silver's parrot and the terraces of New Orleans
I love Mark Twain and the Mississippi steamboats and Abraham
Lincoln's dogs
I love the fields of wheat and corn and the smell of Virginia
tobacco.

But I am not American. Is that enough for the Phantom pilot to turn me back to the Stone Age!
I need neither oil, nor America herself, neither the elephant nor the donkey.
Leave me, pilot, leave my house roofed with palm fronds and this wooden bridge.
I need neither your Golden Gate nor your skyscrapers.
I need the village not New York.
Why did you come to me from your Nevada desert, soldier armed to the teeth?
Why did you come all the way to distant Basra where fish used to swim by our doorsteps.
Pigs do not forage here. I only have these water buffaloes lazily chewing on water lilies.
Leave me alone soldier.
Leave me my floating cane hut and my fishing spear.
Leave me my migrating birds and the green plumes.
Take your roaring iron birds and your Tomahawk missiles. I am not your foe.
I am the one who wades up to the knees in rice paddies.
Leave me to my curse.
I do not need your day of doom.

God save America
My home sweet home!

America
let us exchange your gifts.
Take your smuggled cigarettes
and give us potatoes.

Take James Bond's golden pistol
and give us Marilyn Monroe's giggle.
Take the heroin syringe under the tree
and give us vaccines.
Take your blueprints for model penitentiaries
and give us village homes.
Take the books of your missionaries
and give us paper for poems to defame you.
Take what you do not have
and give us what we have.
Take the stripes of your flag
and give us the stars.

Take the Afghani Mujahideen's beard
and give us Walt Whitman's beard filled with butterflies.
Take Saddam Hussain
and give us Abraham Lincoln
or give us no one.

Now as I look across the balcony
across the summer sky, the summery summer
Damascus spins, dizzied among television aerials
then it sinks, deeply, in the stories of the forts
                    and towers
                    and the arabesques of ivory
and sinks, deeply, from Rukn al-Din
then disappears from the balcony.

And now
I remember trees:

the date palm of our mosque in Basra, at the end of Basra
the bird's beak
and a child's secret
a summer feast.
I remember the date palm.
I touch it. I become it, when it falls black without fronds
when a dam fell hewn by lightning.
And I remember the mighty mulberry
when it rumbled, butchered with an axe ...
to fill the stream with leaves
and birds
and angels
and green blood.
I remember when pomegranate blossoms covered the sidewalks,
the students were leading the workers' parade ...

The trees die
pummelled
dizzied,
not standing
the trees die.

> God save America
> My home sweet home!

We are not hostages, America
and your soldiers are not God's soldiers ...
We are the poor ones, ours is the earth of the drowned gods
the gods of bulls

the gods of fires
the gods of sorrows that intertwine clay and blood in a song ...
We are the poor, ours is the god of the poor
who emerges out of the farmers' ribs
hungry
and bright
and raises heads up high ...
America, we are the dead
Let your soldiers come
Whoever kills a man, let him resurrect him
We are the drowned ones, dear lady

We are the drowned
Let the water come

Saadi Youssef
Translated by Khaled Mattawa

Death as everyday life

Cynthia Cockburn

In words and photographs Cynthia Cockburn explores our discomfort and anxiety around the lifeless body.

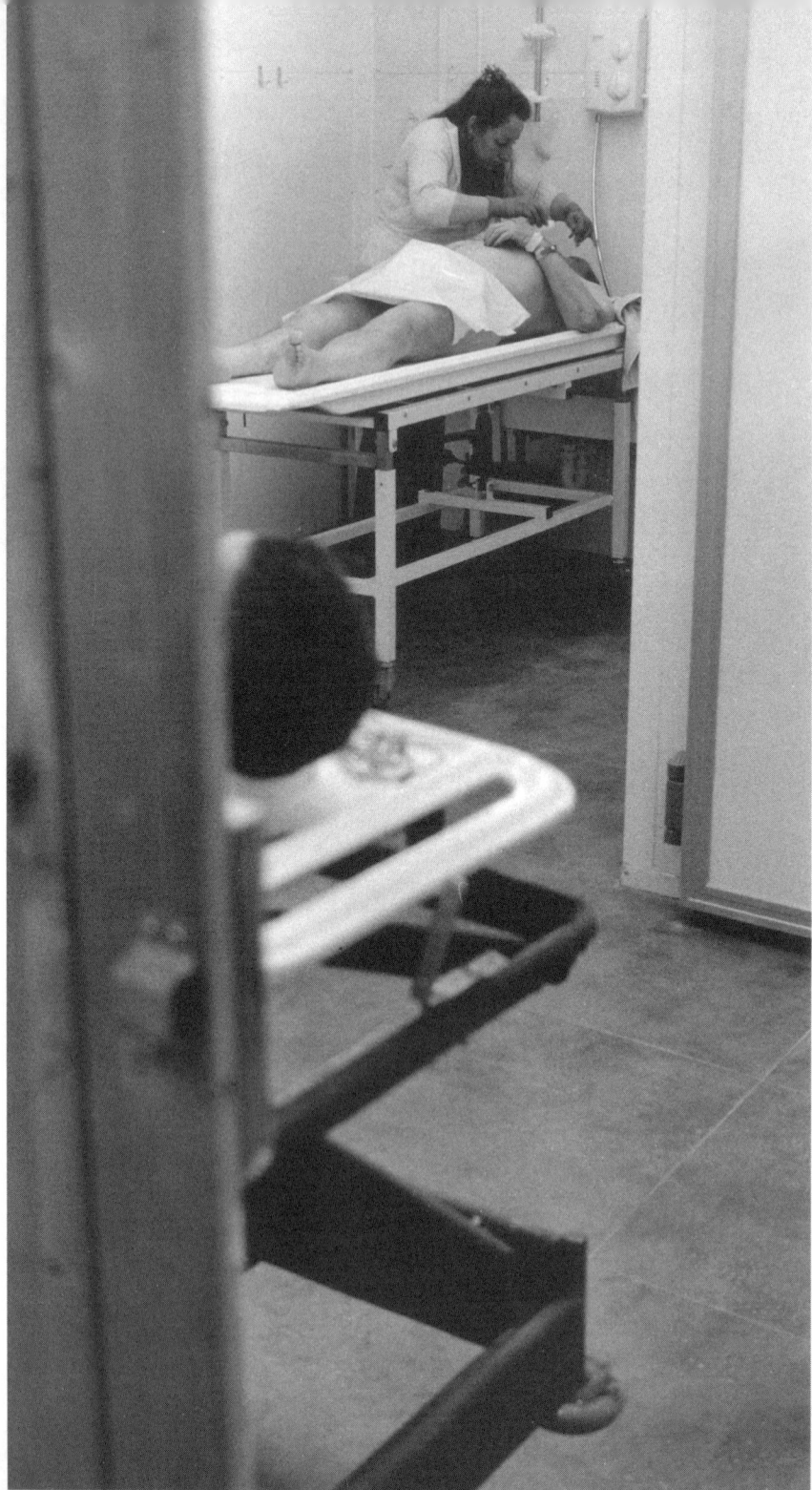

In house windows along certain streets in north London last winter there was a blooming of orange posters. 'Community not Death', they read, and 'No Morgue'. They were the response of a Tufnell Park residents' group to the request by a local business for planning permission to install a refrigerator, two metres high and wide, in an existing shed in a small industrial estate onto which their gardens backed. The fridge was designed to hold up to eight bodies of recently dead people. For Green Endings ('*Funerals of your choice*' - www.greenendings. co.uk), it would be helpful to have a fridge of their own, so they would no longer need to hire mortuary space, at some cost and inconvenience, from the large undertaking firms with whom they compete.

The flurry of rage and protest this planning proposal evoked died down after the council committee granted permission, and the fridge began to receive its intended cargo. But doorstep conversations during a period of canvassing before the decision was taken revealed an interesting polarisation of opinion. Some people felt strongly that 'in the community' was precisely the place an undertaking business ought to be - along with ante-natal classes, playgroups, doctors and dentists' surgeries, opticians shops and Help the Aged second-hand stores. Other people felt it to be somehow foul, unhygienic and even scary that deceased people should be permitted to linger around 'in the community'. Although some local home-owners actually felt and expressed this disgust and fear on their own account, it has to be said that in many cases they were projecting these feelings onto potential house-buyers. They were afraid the presence of the small mortuary would bring down the sale price of their homes. Either way, the negativity was expressed not only in posters and a fierce campaign in the local press, but in aggressive graffiti, verbal abuse and spitting in the street.

What came to light here was a pervasive fear of death. Not so much a fear of dying, which is perennial and explicit in most of us, but a submerged horror concerning *the* dead, corpses. They only remain in the world of the living long enough for the legal requirements to be satisfied and the mourners assembled, but those few days between the last breath and the moment the body can be passed into the grave or the big heat seem to cause anxiety. The disquiet is felt most among those who have little relation to the deceased, who are simply in their vicinity. The people closest to the dead, on the contrary, are often reluctant to let the body go from bedroom or hospice. Both reactions, though, express

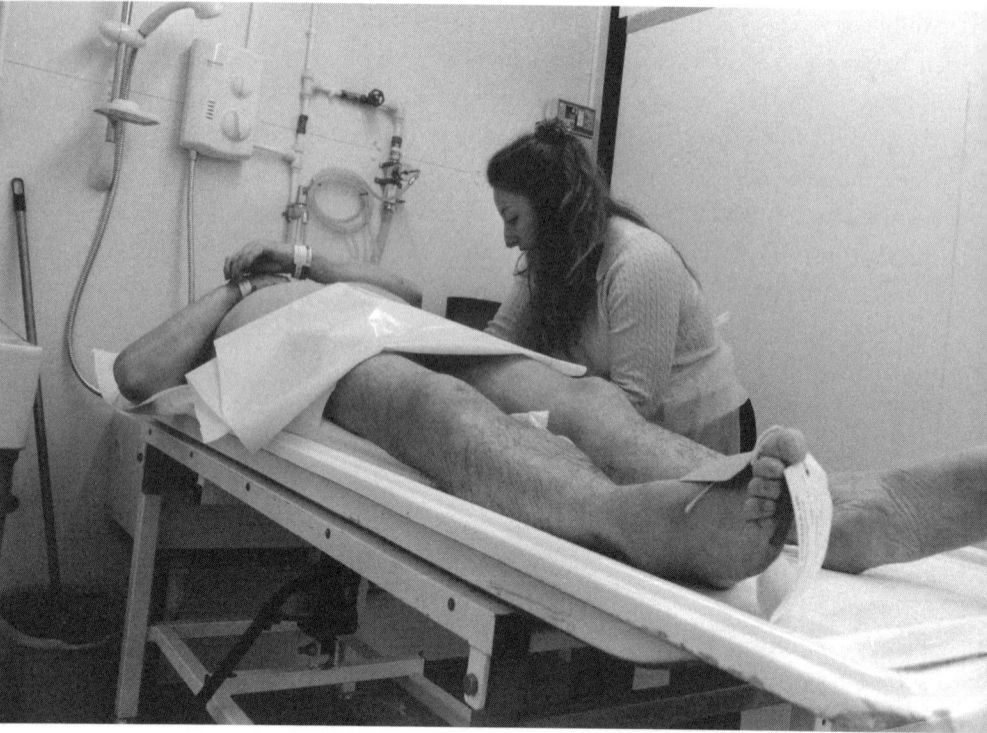

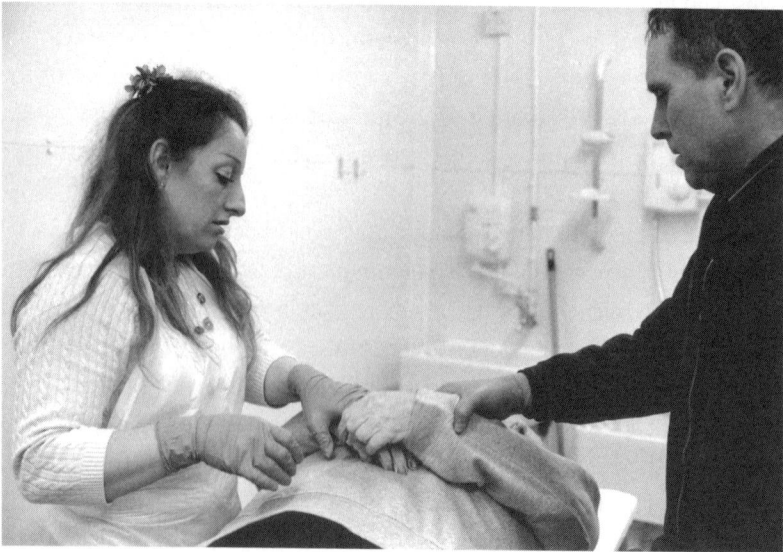

doubts about exactly when and how death occurs.

There is a deep suspicion that life may not obey the ruling of the doctor who palpates the fading pulse and states 'heartbeat and breathing have ceased - I pronounce this person dead'. The uncertainty may be, on the wholesome and humanist side, an understandable hunch that consciousness may not switch off like a light bulb but continue in some attenuated way as the body cools to the ambient temperature, the lively cells slow their dance, and putrefaction begins (36 hours in temperate conditions, estimate Green & Green in their excellent handbook *Dealing with Death*[1]). On the uglier side, the uncertainty is whipped to a frenzy by zombie films and ghost stories, so that we fear these non-dead may yet stir and rise up from their mortuary gurneys when our back is turned.

One of the ambiguities inherent in deadness is 'whose' the body is. There are some wonderful manifestations of this in the Department of Health's manual for mortuary staff, *Care and Respect in Death*.[2] Principle 6 states: 'Patient care does not end with a person's death. Mortuary services provided by NHS trusts are integral to the patient care pathway.' But who exactly is it the Blairite NHS now sees, at the end of the pathway, where the light fades, as patient, as stakeholder? The dead, or the bereaved living? Principle 2 says '…policy and practice in the mortuary will demonstrate respect towards those who have died, towards bereaved relatives and in the way people's bodies are cared for.' People's bodies? Am I the 'people' they have in mind, as in 'my body when I'm dead'. Or will it then be mine no longer? Maybe the 'people' to whom the apostrophe ascribes ownership are my family and friends, who live on to take responsibility for the body in question. And what identity do they ascribe to the body? When do they stop saying, for instance, 'who will move Mary' and start saying 'who will move Mary's body'?. I think, by the time the ashes are stacked in the crematorium's white plastic jars, they are, for most of us, Mary's ashes, not Mary. But to reach that point, a transition has had to occur, an acknowledgment that our perception of the remains has changed. In changing, they have become less of a worry.

Thomas Lynch, US poet and undertaker, wrote about all this ambiguity. A lot

---

1. Jennifer Green and Michael Green, *Dealing with Death: A Handbook of Practices, Procedures and Law* (2nd Edition), Jessica Kingsley 2006.
2. Department of Health, *Care and Respect in Death: Good Practice Guidance for NHS Mortuary Staff*, Department of Health 2006.

of anxious thought goes into doing with the body what the dead person would have wanted - no autopsy for instance. But the central fact of his business he said, is that

> there is nothing, once you are dead, that can be done *to you* or *for you* or *with you* or *about you* that will do you any good or any harm … any damage or decency we do accrues to the living, to whom your death happens, if it really happens to anyone … Which is not to say that the dead do not matter. They do. They do. Of course they do.[3]

If health services and undertakers dwell helpfully on appropriate behaviour towards dead bodies, reflecting Lynch's insistence that they 'matter', the materiality is seldom recognised in intellectual takes on death, which fix the gaze rather on lofty ontological questions concerning mortality and immortality, the fear not of the dead as 'other' but the self's fear of non-being.

Zygmunt Bauman is a man of many words, and reasoning is his trade. But reason, he finds, stalls at death. 'Death is the ultimate defeat of reason, since reason cannot "think" death - not what we know death to be like: the thought of death is - and is bound to remain - *a contradiction in terms*.'[4] For him the Tufnell Park *fracas* might have been due less to apprehension about the way the too-local dead might smell, or block the drains, than to our lack of a language in which to talk about death at all. Modernity, he says, is geared only to the project of life. We know only a manipulating, instrumental language, geared to action.

In my recent exploration of writings on death, however, I stumbled on one marvellous piece of work, inserted exactly into this space where intellect addresses the body and its transitions without flinching, without seeking the escape hatch into metaphysics. In *Lost Bodies*, Laura Tanner explores death through texts, poetry, fiction, autobiography.[5] But she stays with the material, with 'the impossibility of disentangling the living subject from a lost body'. She recognises how not just the loss of a personality, but

---

3. Thomas Lynch, *The Undertaking: Life Studies from the Dismal Trade*, Vintage 1998.
4. Zygmunt Bauman, *Mortality, Immortality and Other Life Strategies*, Polity 1992, p13.
5. Laura E. Tanner, *Lost Bodies: Inhabiting the Borders of Life and Death*, Cornell University Press 2006, p4.

the stillness and coldness of the body itself is a source of terrible grief. We mourn *with* our own bodies and *for* the body as it goes through the sequential processes of deadness. We long to touch, but fear to touch, this body. So - well-meant counselling that dwells on 'happy memories', mere images and representations, sells us short, betrays us. These counsellors should read Maurice Merleau-Ponty to understand how difficult it is to disentwine bodies, how intercorporeally we live and die.[6]

That *Lost Bodies* is written by a woman may be no accident. Quite often, though not always, death features a sexual division of labour. Women are the ones who do immanence for a living (washing bodies) and men those who do transcendence (inventing civilisation to assure immortality). That's the way

---

6. Maurice Merleau-Ponty (ed. Claude Lefort), *The Visible and the Invisible*, Northwestern University Press 1968.

Simone de Beauvoir saw things of course.[7] Women stuck in immanence, up to the elbows in soap suds; men chasing the grail of transcendence, composing operas, climbing the mountain to speak to god, doing metaphysics. (Understandably angry at the way women are short-changed in this, aspiring to more transcendence for the second sex, de Beauvoir herself seems to belittle the kitchen and bathroom duties, flesh-care.)

In Christian cultures in the past, while women washed, clothed and kept watch over the body after death, male priests interceded for the soul. The undertaker who carried the body to the churchyard was likely to be another man, often a carpenter, for whom coffin-making was part of the family craft of joinery. In Victorian times the whole thing became rigidly formalised, a smooth performance enacted by po-faced men, a drama in black barathea, oak and brass. Today the

---

7. Simone De Beauvoir, *The Second Sex*, Penguin Books 1972 (first published 1949).

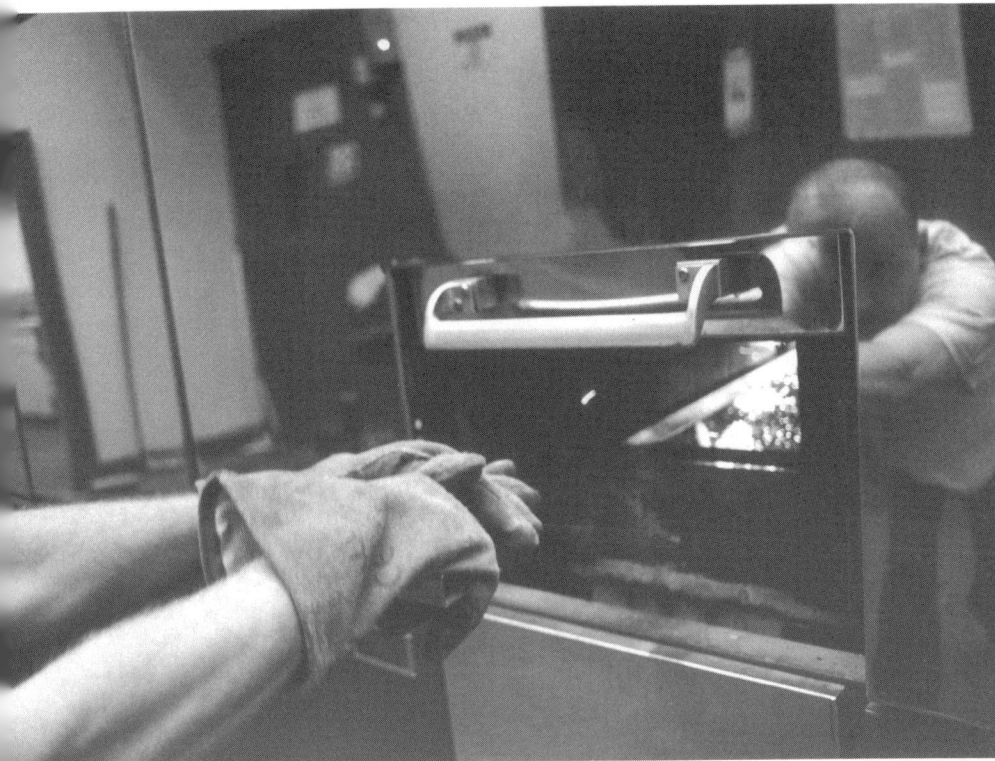

traditional forms are being subverted by a movement of people who resent the domineering presence of church and undertaking cartel, overshadowing the relationship between people and their newly dead loved ones.

The movement, born in 1993 with the publication of *The Natural Death Handbook*,[8] is concerned with both before- and after-death moments. It follows half a century after the 'natural childbirth' movement, and, like the latter, has been a recovery of control, letting non-professionals and particularly women, back into the field. Green Endings is characteristic of the new undertaking, a breakaway from the market grip of the big national companies that have branches in every city and suburb. They offer an environment-friendly service, avoid embalming, use no harmful chemicals, and offer biodegradable coffins - bamboo or willow ones you can weave with flowers, cardboard ones you can paint or write on. They reassure people that, with support, they can learn how to do the death thing for themselves. Death certificates, permissions to dispose of the body, Forms B, C and F, are demystified. Although provision is made for all kinds of religious belief, an undertaker such as this is most popular with people who want to evade institutionalised religion and express their spirituality in their own way.

---

8. *The Natural Death Handbook* (4th edition), published by the Natural Death Centre, London, www.naturaldeathcentre.co.uk.

Roslyn Cassidy, who set up Green Endings in 2000, is a chartered physiotherapist, used to bodies, their functioning, their feel. She has business skills, stretched to the full by the complex logistics of funeral planning and performance. And she's an experienced counsellor and knows the importance of good listening. Responding to a phone call from someone who's just experienced a death, she will make a home visit 'to get a feel' of how best to help them find, in this bad moment, some experience that will be of lasting value. She listens carefully to what they want, sets out the choices available to them.

Sympathetic contact is intrinsic to the job, whether it's with the living or the dead. Roslyn and her assistants Angela, Andrew and Ben are all able to perform what used to be called 'the last offices' or help family or friends to do so. Together they wash the body of the dead, shampoo hair, trim nails, dress in favourite clothes, stow them in that contested fridge. 'How *can* you do this work?' people sometimes ask. Andrew says, 'Bodies? It's not an issue for me. You see them everyday, *people in a state of death*.' Angela, who is mother to three school-age children and commutes an hour and a half to this job each day because she loves it, says 'I was a terminal-care nurse. Then, I held their hands as they died. Here, I've just followed them through the door. I'm tending them on the other side.'

The body may be carried back home to the family, for a night or a day, if that's what is wished. The team will help organise an event where you (in your brightest clothes, no black necessary) may bear the coffin at the crematorium or the burial site. They'll help you make the funeral an occasion to which you bring your own music and poetry, photographs and other precious things, and in which all family and friends, including children, are creatively involved. If a celebrant is wanted to take a lead in the event, she or he may be humanist (i.e. atheist) or Buddhist or just someone known and trusted. It might even, at a stretch, be a priest.

There is little that can be done to mitigate the shock of the final disposal. The solar temperatures of the furnace, the sight and sound of the sullen earth falling on a gaily painted coffin, in the end there is no avoiding these things. But at least a course has been steered between one kind of alienation and another, between offending the senses too long and sweeping the body out of sight too soon. Between holding on and sending away. Those few important days should have been a pause for the breathless and the still painfully breathing to keep company, for the affinities and differences between them to be felt. The body is not the person, no. But it isn't rubbish either.

***

Warm thanks to Roslyn Cassidy, Andrew Castle, Angela Berriman and Ben Weikinat of Green Endings who let me shadow their work; to Zoe Jones who welcomed me and my camera to the funeral of her brother Sunny; to Kelly Drake who let me join her when she and friends were painting the coffin of her mother, Margaret Drake; and to Paul Jennings who let me photograph him at work at Golders Green crematorium.

NOTES ON CONTRIBUTORS

Valerie Bryson is Professor of Politics at the University of Huddersfield. She has published widely on feminist theory and politics. Her latest book is *Gender and the Politics of Time: Political Theory and Contemporary Debates*, The Policy Press 2007.

Lin Chun is Lecturer in Comparative Politics at the LSE. She is author of *The Transformation of Chinese Socialism*, Duke University Press 2006; and *The British New Left*, Edinburgh University Press 1993.

Cynthia Cockburn is Visiting Professor in the Department of Sociology at City University, London. Her most recent publications are *From Where We Stand: War, Women's Activism and Feminist Analysis*, Zed Books 2007; *The Line: Women, Partition and the Gender Order in Cyprus*, Zed Books 2004; *The Postwar Moment: Militaries, Masculinities and International Peacekeeping*, Lawrence and Wishart 2002. She is active in the international antimilitarist network *Women in Black*.

Faisal Devji is Assistant Professor of History at the New School University, New York. His book on the role of militancy and morality in the globalisation of Islam is *Landscapes of the Jihad: Militancy, Morality, Modernity*, Hurst 2005.

Nira Yuval-Davis is a Professor at the University of East London. She has written extensively on theoretical and empirical aspects of nationalism, racism, fundamentalism, citizenship and gender relations in Britain & Europe, Israel and other Settler Societies. Her latest books are *Warning Signs of Fundamentalisms*, WLUML 2004, and *The Situated Politics of Belonging*, Sage 2006.

Jane Duran was brought up in the USA and in Chile, and moved to England in 1966. Her first collection *Breathe Now, Breathe* (Enitharmon) won the 1995 Forward Prize for Best First Collection. Her latest book *Coastal* is published by Enitharmon. The Poetry Translation centre can be contacted at poet@soas.ac.uk

Gagan Gill was born in Delhi in 1959. She gave up a successful career in journalism in order to concentrate on her poetry. She has published four collections of poetry and one volume of prose.

Toeti Heraty Noerhadi Roosseno was born in 1933 in Bandung. She is a feminist poet whose most recent work includes Nostalgi Transendensi (1995), Calong Arang (2000), Hidup Mati Sang Pengarang (2000) and A Time A Season (2003). She is Professor in Philosophy at the University of Indonesia, and manages the Cemara 6 Gallery and her family's business enterprise.

Ramin Jahanbegloo is Rajni Kothari Professor of Democracy at the Centre for the Study of Developing Societies in Delhi. The author of twenty books including, Iran - Between Tradition and Modernity (Rowman & Littlefield 2004), and Talking India: Conversations with Ashis Nandy (Oxford University Press 2006), he is one of the founders of the journal Goft-o-gu (Dialogue) in Tehran. For a selection of his writings, see www.iranproject.info/articles/articles.asp.

Richard Jones is Professor of Physics at the University of Sheffield. He is an experimental nanoscientist and was elected a Fellow of the Royal Society in 2006. He is the author, with Alison Geldart and Stephen Wood, of the 2003 report for the Economic and Social Research Council: The Social and Economic Challenges of Nanotechnology, and the 2007 follow-up report Nanotechnology: from the Science to the Social. His book, Soft Machines: nanotechnology and life, is published by Oxford University Press. He is chair of the Nanotechnology Engagement Group, and Senior Strategic Advisor for Nanotechnology for the Engineering and Physical Sciences Research Council.

Ken Livingstone is Mayor of London.

Nick Mahony is a doctoral student with the Open University's Centre for Citizenship, Identities and Governance. His research is currently exploring a sample of recent public participation experiments undertaken by local government, social movement and media organisations. The research compares the different ideas of politics and democracy, spatial and temporal practices, divisions of deliberative labour, and forms of interaction brought into being in each of these three sites of innovation.

Doreen Massey is a founding editor of *Soundings*.

Khaled Mattawa is the author of two books of poems, *Zodiac of Echoes*, Ausable Press 2003, and *Ismailia Eclipse*, Sheep Meadow Press 1995. He has translated five volumes of Arabic poetry, and is co-editor of two anthologies of Arab American literature. Born in Benghazi, Libya, he teaches in the creative writing programme at the University of Michigan, Ann Arbor.

Janet Newman is Professor of Social Policy at the Open University. Her work centres on analyses of governance, policy and politics; with a particular focus on public services and the public sphere. Publications include *The Managerial State*, with John Clarke, 1997; *Modernising Governance* 2001; and *Remaking governance*, 2005. Recent research includes studies of deliberative forums (*Power, participation and political renewal*, with M. Barnes and H. Sullivan: 2007) and of public service consumerism (*Creating Citizen-*

Consumers, with J.Clarke et al: 2007).

Danny Postel is Senior Editor of openDemocracy.net; Contributing Editor to *Dædalus*, the journal of the American Academy of Arts & Sciences; and a member of the editorial boards of *The Common Review* and *Logos: A Journal of Modern Society & Culture*. He is the author of *Reading 'Legitimation Crisis' in Tehran: Iran and the Future of Liberalism* (Prickly Paradigm Press 2006), from which this interview is excerpted.

Lucy Rosenstein is a senior lecturer in Hindi at the School of Oriental and African Studies, London.

Michael Rustin is a founding editor of *Soundings*.

Jonathan Rutherford is editor of *Soundings*.

Carole Satyamurti's latest collection of poetry is *Stitching the Dark: New and Selected Poems*, Bloodaxe 2005.

Erik Olin Wright is Vilas Distinguished Professor of Sociology at the University of Wisconsin. His academic work has been centrally concerned with reconstructing the Marxist tradition of social theory and research. Since 1992 he has directed *The Real Utopias Project* which explores a range of proposals for new institutional designs that embody emancipatory ideals and yet are attentive to issues of pragmatic feasibility. His latest publications include *Class Counts: Comparative Studies in Class Analysis*, Cambridge University Press 1997; and (with Archon Fung), *Deepening Democracy: institutional innovations in empowered participatory governance*, Verso 2003. See www.ssc.wisc.edu/~wright.

Saadi Youssef was born near Basra, Iraq, in 1934. In 1958 he published his fourth and a now-renowned collection, *51 poems*, following the overthrow of the monarchy in Iraq. He left his country for the second and last time in 1979 and has lived in Syria, Lebanon, Yugoslavia, Yemen, France and Jordan, and for many years in Algeria. He has published more than thirty collections of poetry and has received several literary awards. His poetry has been translated into English most recently by Khaled Mattawa, *Without an Alphabet, Without a Face* (Graywolf Press 2002). He lives in London and is a contributing editor of *Banipal* (www.banipal.co.uk).

compass

DIRECTION FOR
THE DEMOCRATIC LEFT

MEMBERSHIP OFFER

Join Compass and get the
5 *Programme for Renewal*
publications including *The Good
Society* edited by Jonathan
Rutherford and Hetan Shah

The
Good Society

COMPASS PROGRAMME FOR RENEWAL

**For £1 make a stand today for greater equality,
democracy and freedom**

Get 3 month's membership for just £1 when you join
by standing order and receive the five 'Programme for
Renewal' publications. Alternatively you can join online
using Paypal and get £5 off our standard rates at www.
compassonline.org.uk/join.asp.

**New members joining Compass will over the
coming months receive 5 excellent publications**

**Visit our website and join online at
www.compassonline.org.uk**

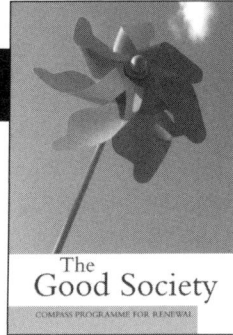

Back Issues

Issue 1 - Launch Issue – Andrew Blake, Beatrix Campbell, Barbara Castle, Simon Edge, Stuart Hall, Fred Halliday, Mae-Wan Ho, Heather Hunt, Lynne Murray, Ingrid Pollard, Michael Rustin Lola Young.

Issue 2 - Law & Justice, editor Bill Bowring - contributors - Kate Markus, Keir Starmer, Ken Wiwa, Kader Asmal, Mike Mansfield, Jonathan Cooper, Ethan Raup, John Griffith, Keith Ewing, Ruth Lister and Anna Coote. Plus Steven Rose/ Jeffrey Weeks/ David Bell.

Issue 3 - Heroes & Heroines - contributors - Barbara Taylor, Jonathan Rutherford, Graham Dawson, Becky Hall, Anna Grimshaw, Simon Edge, Kirsten Notten, Susannah Radstone, Graham Martin and Cynthia Cockburn. Plus Anthony Barnett/ David Donnison/ John Gill and Nick Hallam.

Issue 4 - The Public Good - editor Maureen Mackintosh - contributors - Gail Lewis, Francie Lund, Pam Smith, Loretta Loach, John Clarke, Jane Falkingham, Paul Johnson, Will Hutton, Charlie King, Anne Simpson, Brigid Benson, Candy Stokes, Anne Showstack Sassoon, Sarabajaya Kumar, Ann Hudock, Carlo

Borzaga and John Stewart. Plus Paul Hirst, Grahame Thompson/ Anne Phillips/ Richard Levins

Issue 5 - Media Worlds - editors Bill Schwarz and David Morley - contributors - James Curran, Sarah Benton, Esther Leslie, Angela McRobbie, David Hesmondhalgh, Jonathan Burston, Kevin Robins, Tony Dowmunt and Tim O'Sullivan. Plus Phil Cohen/ Duncan Green/ Cynthia Cockburn.

Issue 6 - 'Young Britain' - editor Jonathan Rutherford - contributors - Jonathan Keane, Bilkis Malek, Elaine Pennicott, Ian Brinkley, John Healey, Frances O'Grady, Rupa Huq, Michael Kenny and Peter Gartside. Plus Miriam Glucksmann/ Costis Hadjimichalis/ Joanna Moncrieff.

Issue 7 - States of Africa - editors Victoria Brittain and Rakiya Omaar - contributors - Basil Davidson/ Augustin Ndahimana Buranga/ Kathurima M'Inoti/ Lucy Hannan/ Jenny Matthews/ Ngugi Wa Mirii/ Kevin Watkins/ Joseph Hanlon/ Laurence Cockcroft/ Joseph Warioba/ Vic Allen and James Motlasi. Plus Bill Schwarz/ Wendy Wheeler/ Dave Featherstone.

Issue 8 - Active Welfare - editor Andrew Cooper - contributors - Rachel Hetherington and Helen Morgan/ John Pitts/ Angela Leopold/ Hassan Ezzedine/ Alain Grevot/ Margherita Gobbi/ Angelo Cassin and Monica Savio. Plus Michael Rustin/ Colette Harris/ Patrick Wright.

Issue 9 - European Left - editor Martin Peterson - contributors - Branka Likic-Brboric/ Mate Szabo/ Leonadis Donskis/ Peter Weinreich/ Alain Caille/ John Crowley/ Ove Sernhede and Alexandra Alund. Plus Angela McRobbie/ Mario Petrucci/ Philip Arestis and Malcolm Sawyer.

Issue 10 - Windrush Echoes - editors Gail Lewis and Lola Young - contributors - Anne Phoenix/ Jackie Kay/ Julia Sudbury/ Femi Franklin/ David Sibley/ Mike Phillips/ Phil Cole/ Bilkis Malek/ Sonia Boyce/ Roshi Naidoo/ Val Wilmer and Stuart Hall. Plus Alan Finlayson/ Richard Moncrieff/ Mario Pianta.

Issue 11 - Emotional Labour - editor Pam Smith - contributors - Stephen Lloyd Smith/ Dympna Casey/ Marjorie Mayo/ Minoo Moallem/ Prue Chamberlayne/ Rosy Martin/ Sue Williams and Gillian Clarke. Plus Andreas Hess/ T. V. Sathyamurthy/ Les Black, Tim Crabbe and John Solomos.

Issue 12 - Transversal Politics - editors Cynthia Cockburn and Lynette Hunter - contributors - Nira Yuval-Davis/ Pragna Patel/ Marie Mulholland/ Rebecca O'Rourke/ Gerri Moriarty/ Jane Plastow and Rosie. Plus Bruno Latour/ Gerry Hassan/ Nick Jeffrey.

Issue 13 - These Sporting Times - editor Andrew Blake - contributors - Carol Smith/ Simon Cook/ Adam Brown/ Steve Greenfield/ Guy Osborne/ Gemma Bryden/ Steve Hawes/ Alan Tomlinson and Adam Locks. Plus Geoff Andrews/ Fred Halliday/ Nick Henry and Adrian Passmore.

Issue 14 - One-Dimensional Politics - editors Wendy Wheeler and Michael Rustin - contributors - Wendy Wheeler/ Michael Rustin/ Dave Byrne/ Gavin Poynter/ Barry Richards and Mario Petrucci. Plus Ann Briggs/ David Renton/ Isaac Balbus/ Laura Dubinsky.

Issue 15 - States of Mind - contributors - Alan Shuttleworth/ Andrew Cooper/ Helen Lucey/ Diane Reay/ Richard Graham and Jennifer Wakelyn. Plus Nancy Fraser/ Stephen Wilkinson/ Mike Waite/ Kate Young.

Issue 16 - Civil Society - editor Andreas Hess - contributors - Jeffrey C. Alexander/ Robert Fine/ Maria

Pia Lara/ William Outhwaite/ Claire Wallace/ Grazyna Kubica-Heller/ Jonathan Freedland. Plus Peter Howells/ G. C.Harcourt/ Emma Satyamurti/ Simon Lewis/ Paulette Goudge/ Tom Wengraf.

Issue 17 - New Political Directions - contributors - Sarah Benton/ Giulio Marcon and Mario Pianta/ Massimo Cacciari/ Sue Tibballs/ Richard Minns/ Ian Taylor/ John Calmore/ Judith Rugg and Michele Sedgwick/ Ruby Millington/ Merilyn Moos/ Jon Bloomfield/ Nick Henry/ Phil Hubbard/ Kevin Ward and David Donnison.

Issue 18 - A Very British Affair - editor Gerry Hassan - contributors - Gerry Hassan/ Jim McCormick/ Mark Perryman/ Katie Grant/ Cathal McCall/ Charlotte Williams/ Paul Chaney/ John Coakley/ Kevin Howard/ Mary-Ann Stephenson/ David T. Evans. Plus Hilary Wainwright/ Angie Birtill/ Beatrix Campbell/ Jane Foot and Csaba Deak/ Geoff Andrews/ Glyn Ford/ Jane Desmarais.

Issue 19 - New World Disorder - contributors Stuart Hall/ Chantal Mouffe/ Gary Younge/ Eli Zaretsky/ David Slater/ Bob Hackett. Plus Jonathan Rutherford/ Anne Costello/ Les Levidow/ Linda McDowell.

Issue 20 - Regimes of Emotion - editors Pam Smith and Stephen Lloyd Smith - contributors - Pam Smith/ Steve Smith/ Arlie Russell Hochschild/ Fiona Douglas/ Maria Lorentzon/ Gay Lee/ Del Loewenthal/ David Newbold/ Bridget Towers/ Stuart Nairn/ Rick Rattue/ Nelarine Cornelius/ Ian Robbins/ Marjorie Mayo/ Trudi James. Plus Nira Yuval Davis, Haim Bresheeth, Lena Jayyusi/ Anita Biressi and Heather Nunn/ Andrew Stevens/ John Grieve Smith & G.C. Harcourt/ Fraser Mcdonald & Andy Cumbers.

Issue 21 - Monsters and Morals - editor Elizabeth B. Silva - contributors - Elizabeth Silva/ Paul Dosh/ Margrit Shildrick/ Janet Fink/ Dale Southerton/ Caroline Knowles. Plus Geoff Andrews/ Tom Kay/ Richard Minns/ Steve Woodhams.

Issue 22 - Fears and Hopes - Irene Bruegel/ Tom Kay/ Paddy Maynes/ Sarah Whatmore and Steve Hinchliffe/ Stuart Hall/ Chantal Mouffe/ Ernesto Laclau/ Geoff Andrews/ Stefan Howald/ David Renton.

Issue 23 - Who needs history? - Geoff Andrews/ Kevin Morgan/ Ilaria Favretto/ John Callaghan/ Maud Bracke and Willie Thompson/ plus Michael Rustin/

Ali Ansari/ Costis Hadjimichalis and Ray Hudson/ Christian Wolmar/ Alan Finlayson/ C. Harcourt/ Laura Agustín.

Issue 24 - A market state? - Stuart Hall/ Alan Finlayson/ Jonathan Rutherford/ Richard Minns/ Renzio Imbeni/ George Irvin/ Adah Kay/ Nora Räthzel/ Michael Saward/ Nora Carlin/ Michael Rustin.

Issue 25 - Rocky times - Geoff Andrews/ Alan Fountain/ Ivor Gaber/ Ash Amin, Doreen Massey, Nigel Thrift/ Gerry Hassan/ Hugh Mackay/ Francisco Domínguez//George Irvin/ Grahame Thompson.

Issue 26 - Resisting Neo-liberalism - Katharine Ainger, Geoff Andrews, Cynthia Cockburn, Jane Foot, Stuart Hall, Jeremy Gilbert, Clare Joy, Sayeed Khan, Jo Littler, Ruth Levitas, Doreen Massey, Catherine Needham, Michael Rustin.

Issue 27 - Public Life - Sarah Benton, Hilary Cottam, Francisco Domínguez, Alan Fountain, Jonathan Hardy, Neal Lawson, Gregor McLennan, Richard Minns, Geoff Mulgan, Robin Murray, Amir Saeed, Judith Squires, Caroline Thomson, Heather Wakefield.

Issue 28 - Frontier Markets - Norman Birnbaum, Alessandra Buonfino, Csaba

Deák, Stefan Howald, George Irvin, Richard Johnson, Brendan Martin, Bronwen Morgan, Liz Moor, Chantal Mouffe, David Purdy, Richard Rorty, Judith Rugg, Michael Rustin, Jonathan Rutherford, Michèle Sedgwick.

Issue 29 - After Identity - Zygmunt Bauman, Sarah Benton, John Callaghan, Paul Gilroy, John Grahl, Tariq Modood, Steve Munby, Andrew Pearmain, Valerie Walkerdine, Wendy Wheeler, Patrick Wright.

Issue 30 - Living Well - Farhad Dalal, John Gittings, Stephan Harrison, Molly Scott Cato, Jacqueline Rose, Michael Rustin, Hetan Shah, Tom Shakespeare, Andrea Westall, Fiona Williams, Ken Worpole, Nira Yuval-Davis.

Issue 31 - Opportunity Knocks - Geoff Andrews, Clive Barnett, Sarah Benton, Sally Davison, Lynda Dyson, Sue Gerhardt, Lawrence Grossberg, Lisa Harker, Jo Littler, Martin McIvor, David Purdy, James Robertson, Kate Soper, Rowan Williams.

Issue 32 - Bare Life - Pat Devine, Faisal Devji, Kurt Jacobsen, Sayeed Khan, Ruth Lister, Doreen Massey, Richard Minns, Janet Newman, Michael Rustin, Jonathan Rutherford, Ejos Ubiribo, Robin Wilson.

Issue 33 - Conviviality - Zygmunt
Bauman, Roshi Naidoo, Alan Finlayson,
Pat Kane, Amir Saeed, Jonathan Keane,
David Wilson, Richard Minns, Richard
Gott, Christoph Bluth, Sue Himmelweit,
Andy Pearmain.

Issue 34 - Ecowars - Vandana Shiva,
Noel Castree, Mary Mellor, Anthony
Jackson, Nigel Mullan, Juliet Schor,
C.J. Campbell, Peter Singer, Jim Mason,
Sarah Benton, Andrew Gamble, Peter
Murphy, Georges Nzongola-Ntalaja,
Bilkis Malek.

Issue 35 - Left futures - Priscilla
Alderson, Zygmunt Bauman, Elisabeth
Beck-Gernsheim, Anna Coote, Patrick
Curry, Jeremy Gilbert, Michael Kenny,
Stewart Lansley, Jackie Law, James
Marriott, David Purdy, Michael Rustin,
Kate Soper

All back issues cost £9.99, plus £2 p&p.
Order from www.lwbooks.co.uk,
or Lawrence & Wishart, 99a Wallis Road, London E9 5LN,
or email to soundings@lwbooks.co.uk.
Tel 020 8533 2506   Fax 020 8533 7369

After Blair
Politics after the New Labour decade
Edited by Gerry Hassan

The Blair era – from the mid 1990s to the mid 2000s – was one of Labour dominance. This book analyses some of the main features of this period, now coming to an end, and asks what the future holds for progressive politics.

Contributors locate the Blair/New Labour legacy within the historical context of Thatcherism and its aftermath, and within a comparative context of previous Labour governments and Labour revisionism. They also look at the ideas that have underpinned developments during this period. An over-arching story of a commitment to socialism once made the compromises of government worthwhile or bearable. *After Blair* asks whether progressives still have a story that can sustain their faith in the future.

Contributors: Zygmunt Bauman, Tom Bentley, Jake Chapman, David Coats, Colin Crouch, Richard Eckersley, Jonathan Freedland, Andrew Gamble, Sue Goss, Gerry Hassan, Alan Finlayson, Edward Fullbrook, Neal Lawson, Ruth Lister, Hetan Shah, Michael Walzer

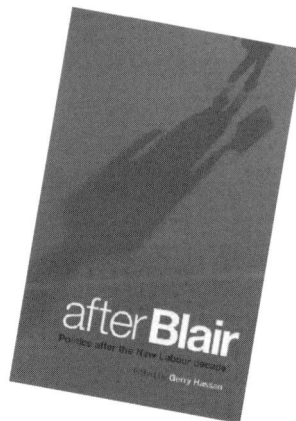

ISBN 978 1905007 417   224 pages   £16.99

For a postfree copy send a cheque to Lawrence and Wishart, PO Box 7701, Latchingdon, Chelmsford, CM3 6WL

Or order from www.lwbooks.co.uk tel: 020 8533 2506 fax: 020 8533 7369 email orders@lwbooks.co.uk